THE CHALLENGES WE FACED,
THE WOMEN WE BECAME

THE CHALLENGES WE FACED, THE WOMEN WE BECAME

ASHLEY BARCROFT

This book represents the personal views and opinions of the interviewees and does not necessarily reflect the positions or opinions of any organization, institution, or individual with which the interviewees are affiliated. The content presented herein is based on the interviewees perspective and interpretation of the subject matter as well as personal experience. Neither the author, the publisher nor any associated parties shall be held responsible for any consequences arising from the opinions or interpretations expressed within this book.

Onion River Press
89 Church Street
Burlington, VT 05401
info@onionriverpress.com
www.onionriverpress.com

ISBN: 978-1-957184-77-7
Library of Congress Control Number: 2024919624

Contents

Introduction

During carefree summer days growing up, stories began compiling in my mind more than ever. As an avid reader now free of the routine and order of school, I lost myself in the books I read, growing deep connections to both fictional and real people. I quickly became intrigued by the idea of sharing stories and the power they can have over us. Through the stories I consumed, I began to think more deeply about how every person has struggles, yet as a society, we typically only see the surface of someone's life. When we only see what someone wants to present to society or the specific mold they're trying to embody, we are no longer talking about the common challenges that we keep hidden out of fear of being unheard or judged. They stay hidden beneath the surface we show to the world.

I realized that the stories that stuck with me all managed to break through that surface. It requires immense strength to be vulnerable, to be honest, and to show a willingness to share and come forward despite a fear of the unknown. When more of these strong voices are heard, we get a better grasp of the human experience and the diverse range of challenges that we can face depending on the life we're born into. Although these challenges can be systemic or caused by others, I realized through listening to these stories that what we do have control over—how we face our challenges and bounce back from difficulties—can help us grow in ways we would never expect.

I began searching for more stories, specifically ones by strong women who have faced unique challenges. I sought out women who I wanted to learn more from, whether they were already successful at sharing their story with the world or if they hadn't yet had the chance to make their voice heard. I thought about the impact of diverse perspectives on my life and knew what those stories could do for others as well. Soon, I drafted a letter outlining what I hoped my book would be and began reaching out to these women so that I could hear their stories firsthand and compile them into a book.

When I embarked on this journey of interviewing women to share their stories of overcoming adversity, I didn't expect much. I thought I would reach out and hear from no one, given that as I am writing this I am 17 and just starting my career as a young journalist. But I was wrong; my expectations were quickly exceeded. Women whom I have admired and whose stories have inspired me responded with kindness and generosity that I have profound appreciation for. I knew these stories would give hope to people who feel isolated or who need inspiration. My goal from the start with the publication of *The Challenges We Faced, The Women We Became* has been to help people in difficult situations better understand that they are not alone in what they are going through. It also has been to spread greater awareness surrounding the fact that accomplished and successful women around the world have also endured similar challenges but were able to find a way to overcome them and become who they are today. I hope this book will be a source of comfort, inspiration, and newfound self-belief for anyone who is struggling to combat their individual challenges and hoping to learn from others' experiences.

1

Dr. Jocelyn Bell Burnell

Dr. Jocelyn Bell Burnell is an astrophysicist from Northern Ireland who discovered the first radio pulsars in 1967. In 1974, the Nobel Prize for Physics was awarded for this discovery, but Professor Bell Burnell was not named among the recipients. Many people protested this decision given the controversy that arose over the subpar treatment of women in science, yet Professor Bell Burnell herself indicated that it was uncommon for a graduate student to receive such an award at the time. In 2018, she received the Special Breakthrough Prize in Fundamental Physics—a 3 million dollar award.

Why did I want to interview Dr. Jocelyn Bell Burnell?

Dr. Bell Burnell is the quintessential example of a woman who demonstrated maturity in the manner with which she handled an unfair decision. The failure to recognize her achievement was not free from controversy; it reflected a significant gender-based obstacle that she faced in her professional career when she was not recognized for her pioneering achievement in science. I wanted to learn more about how that experience might have shaped her professional approach and outlook in the years after the Nobel Prize was awarded.

Ashley: What was your childhood like, and what led you to become passionate about astrophysics?

Dr. Bell Burnell: Growing up in Northern Ireland, I was the eldest of four children. My father was an architect, and my mother looked after us. I was born during the Second World War in a household that was housing several Jewish refugees from Germany. I went to the local all-girls school until age 13, and then I went away to boarding school in the North of England. It was a significant change in environment for me, but I looked forward to furthering my education. I had a battle to do science in the Northern Irish school. Girls did domestic science, meaning they learned how to be good housewives. The bulk of what I was meant to learn was needlework and cookery. The boys got to do science. I knew I wanted to do science.

My parents also wanted me to do science. They advocated for me, protesting to the school that I should be allowed to join the class. By the time of the second lesson, there were three girls doing science, along with 27 boys. One of the other girls had a father who was a doctor, and the other was her cousin. It was rare for parents to support their daughters going into science at the time. My parents saw the value of providing girls with a scientific education. We did physics in the first term. I absolutely loved it. I quickly rose to the top of my class, surprising my teacher and fellow classmates. In the following term, we did chemistry, and in the summer term, we did biology. I knew that I wanted to continue studying physics, and I continued doing well in it as well as mathematics. I became interested in astrophysics. Despite people finding it peculiar, I pursued an honors undergraduate physics degree after leaving school.

Ashley: What was your experience as a woman in university life? Did men at the university view you differently?

Dr. Bell Burnell: I went to the University of Glasgow in Scotland. Once again, I was an exception. Out of the 50 students in my class, I was the only female. I felt too visible. The attitude towards female students was fairly rough at that time. There were sexual undertones in the way men viewed women. I think men saw young women as potential girlfriends more than fellow students. I took care not to be the girlfriend of anybody in my class.

After getting my undergraduate degree, I attended the University of Cambridge to receive my doctorate. When I got to Cambridge, again, nearly all the students were men. The position of women in the university was a bit precarious. We had to behave absolutely impeccably. Senior women were afraid that if some of the female students misbehaved, men would think even less of women, so I continued to work very hard. This is when I accidentally discovered a scientific breakthrough: pulsars, a new kind of star.

Ashley: Could you walk me through your discovery of pulsars? How did you discover them?

Dr. Bell Burnell: Prior to the discovery, my thesis advisor, Tony Hewish, had an idea to build a radio telescope to find quasars, a massive celestial object admitting large amounts of energy. The telescope would help me detect quasars by using radio wavelengths to detect distant objects in space. It took two years to build. I picked up a radio interference that didn't look natural. I worked with my thesis advisor to figure out what this was, and I then found another radio interference in a different part of the sky. Then a third and a fourth. It became clear to me that it was some different kind of star or galaxy up in the sky giving out these radio waves going "bleep bleep bleep." It was a relief to find the second one in a different part of the sky. When you only have one curious phenomenon, you suspect your equipment was misbehaving, or you were doing something wrong. You need more evidence. So, finding pulsars in different parts of the sky, each bleeping at their own rate, told me there was a new kind of star.

Ashley: What are pulsars?

Dr. Bell Burnell: It was a very compact star, almost the size of a planet, yet it had the same weight as a star. The sun spins once every 27 days, whereas pulsars spin once every 30 seconds to a minute. They are quite good clocks as well. They were unusual and interesting. Now that we know thousands of them, they are very good probes for studying the universe.

Ashley: So, once you discovered the pulsar, where did you go from there?

Dr. Bell Burnell: After my discovery, I began writing my thesis. I got married and began following my husband around the country. He got a promotion by moving to different parts of the country, and I got astronomy jobs where I could. I started in radio astronomy, and my next job was in gamma-ray astronomy. After that, I did X-ray astronomy and then infrared astronomy. So, I did astronomy across a lot of the spectrum.

Ashley: When did the Nobel Prize award come out? What was your reaction when you found out the news?

Dr. Bell Burnell: I had just started work studying X-ray astronomy, using a satellite above the Earth's atmosphere to do so. Our satellite launched early that morning, and we went to our offices to get on with our jobs. Suddenly, someone came roaring into my office, asking me, "Have you heard the news?" I was worried something had happened with the satellite. I was wrong. The Nobel Prize for Physics was announced. It was awarded jointly to Martin Ryle, the head of the Cambridge Radio Astronomy Group, and my former advisor, Tony Hewish, for "his decisive role in the discovery of pulsars." I was pleased that this was the first time the physics prize was going to anything astronomical. It was a huge step. I knew having broken that barrier, future Nobel Prizes for physics could go to astronomy topics, and indeed they have.

I went to Stockholm for the award as Tony Hewish's guest. Looking back on it, I think the Nobel Prize staff was anxious knowing my contributions. They were probably afraid I would've protested it. I did feel I was a bit overlooked, having been a female graduate student at the time of the discovery, but I was pleased astronomy was being viewed with such high importance, no matter who the prize went to.

Ashley: After this, where did your job pick up? What were you working on at this point?

Dr. Bell Burnell: I continued X-ray astronomy, which proved to be extremely exciting. We kept discovering new things that were sending out X-rays. My job was to find a student to analyze the satellite's data, keeping me busy. We made new discoveries and were successful.

Ashley: Do you have a closing message regarding your ability to overcome your challenge?

Dr. Bell Burnell: Almost every year since my discovery, there has been some prize or medal that I have been awarded. The Nobel Prize has great prestige, meaning sometimes people may think you are too high up to be approached. So, I think I have done very well along the lines of not receiving the Nobel Prize. I recently received a prize from the Breakthrough Foundation of 3 million dollars, which I donated to support those under-represented in physics.

Being a woman, having a child, and following my husband around the country has not made my life simple. I learned to be flexible and take advantage of opportunities that I am passionate about.

What I learned from interviewing Dr. Jocelyn Bell Burnell

When faced with a setback in life, sometimes our instinctive response is to feel resentment or anger towards the situation. But the moment we put the setback into perspective and focus on what it is we can control, we can learn rather than be diminished by the situation.

Dr. Bell Burnell's account reminds us that a measured response to setbacks in our lives can be an extraordinary motivational force and inspirational example for others who find themselves in similar circumstances. Rather than becoming permanently embittered as a result of this experience early in her career, Dr. Bell Burnell channeled this to continue her contributions to science.

2

Dr. Gladys Kalema-Zikusoka

Dr. Gladys Kalema-Zikusoka is a wildlife veterinarian from Uganda who is the founder and CEO of the non-profit and NGO Conservation Through Public Health, which aims to improve the health of people and wildlife by educating communities on ways to balance human needs with conservation concerns. Dr Gladys Kalema-Zikusoka also oversaw and conducted research with a team looking into the first outbreak of gorilla scabies. She wrote the book *Walking with Gorillas: The Journey of an African Wildlife Vet*, which tells the story of her conservation journey. Her award-winning work made her one of BBC's 100 most influential women in 2023.

Why did I want to interview Dr. Gladys Kalema-Zikusoka?

Along with others in my generation, I recognize that now, more than ever, there is an immense concern about climate change. Questions like: *"What will life be like for my children if I decide to have them?"* and, *"Will I eventually have to move because of wildfires or other climate related concerns?"* are at the forefront of my mind. I hoped to gain from Dr. Gladys Kalema-Zikusoka the knowledge of how one community can recognize the benefits of sustaining gorillas, a vital part of their environment, and use its own workforce to build up tourism to help their economy and livelihoods. It was also Dr. Gladys Kalema-Ziku-soka's tenacity and drive to educate and give back to her community by saving gorillas that caught my attention.

Ashley: What was your childhood like growing up?

Dr. Gladys Kalema-Zikusoka: I'd say that my childhood was different from most people's in Uganda because I grew up in a family of six, and all my siblings were much older than me. My sister, who I followed, was five years older than me, so we were just outside each other's age bracket to play with one another. I got very interested in animals because my older brother, who was 10 years older than me, was bringing stray cats and dogs home, and I fell in love with them. The pets became my friends and whenever they got sick, I would always miss school just to take them to the vet at the nearby animal clinic. I really loved school because that's when I could get to see other kids. One time, we got an unusual pet, which was owned by the Cuban ambassador across the road: a monkey, which they called Poncho, a Cuban name. He was a very naughty monkey. Poncho used to like coming home, pulling the cats' and dogs' tails and stealing mangoes and bananas from the kitchen. Then one time I was playing the piano, and I felt like I wasn't alone. I realized Poncho was watching me. I thought, *Okay, let me see what this monkey can do.* So, I left the room, and he came and played one note with one finger. I thought, *He is so intelligent. Not only do his fingers look like mine, he can also play the piano.* That's when I started getting really fascinated with primates. I must have been around eight or nine when that happened.

I grew up in the Capital City of Uganda. I didn't even grow up in a national park. However, I got the chance to set up a wildlife club in high school, and that's when my passion for conservation really began. It was so exciting. We held debating clubs with the school children, and then we organized a school trip to a national park—one of the first three national parks created in Uganda. When we got to Queen

Elizabeth National Park, while it was very exciting to be there, I was disappointed that there was not much wildlife because a lot had been poached during the President Idi Amin era, and the wildlife had gone to the neighboring Democratic Republic of Congo to run away from the troubles. Lions had either left because there wasn't enough to eat or had been killed. We couldn't even do a walking safari because it wasn't safe enough to walk. So, I thought, *Why don't I become a vet who brings back the wildlife?* Having grown up with many pets at home, I also thought about being a vet working with all sorts of wildlife. When I started vet school in London at the Royal Veterinary College, University of London, I had an opportunity to come back home and work with wildlife. So that really helped to keep nurturing my passion to work with wildlife.

Ashley: How did you eventually make the discovery of parasite transmission from humans to gorillas when studying that?

Dr. Gladys Kalema-Zikusoka: When I was at the vet school in London, I came back to Uganda on holiday, and I worked with captive chimpanzees in the zoo and with chimpanzees in the wild. I also got to work with gorillas in the wild, looking at their fecal samples and the presence of bacteria. This made me want to become a full-time wildlife vet. I wrote a letter to the Executive Director of the Uganda National Parks about hiring me as their first veterinarian to look after their wildlife. I said, "You need a vet. This is what a vet can do to help wildlife." He was convinced and wrote back to me and said, "Come back; you have a job." I was so excited to start working at Uganda National Parks. But when I got to Uganda, I found that a lot of conservation biologists never really wanted anyone to touch animals because, in those days, no one really touched animals. But we all agreed that because gorillas are so few in number, they could easily be disrupted by humans, and they already had been disrupted by humans. We needed to intervene if the animals were endangered. And so, one of the first cases I had, nine months into the job, was when I got a message that the gorillas were losing hair and developing white scaly skin. I wondered where it could have come from, and I asked myself, *What is the most common skin disease in people?*

Because I knew that we are so closely related to the gorillas, [I knew] we could easily make each other sick. And that's why the Executive Director was convinced to hire me, because tourism had begun, and they were concerned that tourists would bring a flu or other respiratory disease like COVID-19 to the gorillas. When I spoke to a medical doctor about the symptoms in the gorillas, she said the most common skin disease in people in Uganda is scabies or sarcoptic mange because low-income groups of people don't bathe and wash their clothes often. And with mites: the spread between people and mites happens easily, and there is always scratching when someone gets scabies. I thought, *Because of the way I was trained in the UK, [I knew] people never got scabies because it's a developed country.* Occasionally, they'll pick it up from their pets, but they rarely got scabies.

I carried ivermectin with me, which works well with skin diseases like scabies. I just hoped that it was not ringworm, because you have to put cream on every day till it gets better. You can't really do that with wild animals. And so, when we got to Bwindi, it ended up being scabies. So, we checked the gorillas, and we found out that it came from the local communities. Gorillas go outside the park to eat people's banana plants, and they come into contact with dirty clothing, which can be infected with scabies mites, and the mites pass through the group. So, we realized that you couldn't keep the gorillas healthy without improving the health of their human neighbors. The reason why gorillas kept going out is because they had lost their fear of people. They went back to places where they used to range before the forest was cut down and the found banana trees and eucalyptus trees that people were encouraged to plant so they didn't have to cut trees in the forest, and the gorillas liked the bark. Gorillas actually prefer the stem of the banana tree to the fruit because they like the moisture inside the stem. So, people put out scarecrows with dirty clothing to scare away gorillas, baboons, birds, and other wildlife. That's the reason I thought, *Why not start a nonprofit that improves the health of the people around the National Park?* so they don't make the gorillas sick, but also so that they support conservation, because we're addressing a basic human need, which is healthcare. And so, that's how we started helping: integrating human health and conservation.

Ashley: How did you begin educating your community on why conservation is important? What struggles did you find in educating them, if any?

Dr. Gladys Kalema-Zikusoka: Once we made the discovery, everybody turned to me, being the only veterinarian in the organization, to start health education workshops. The local community [was] not only exposed to dirty clothing on scarecrows, but people [were] openly defecating in their garden. People [were] not covering their rubbish heaps. There's lots of areas the gorillas can get exposed to when they enter community land. That was a turning point in my life. We developed some brochures on the risks of human and gorilla disease transmission. When I went out to talk to the community about how people made gorillas sick, I was about to tell them how to prevent this, and the ranger touched my arm and said, "Let's just hear what they have to say." They came up with much better suggestions than what I was proposing for them, much more varied. And I thought, *Wow.* I then realized the best way to carry out conservation education is to get people to own the solution to the conservation issue they're addressing. That was a huge eye-opener for me.

A very humbling event, but a very important eye opener—a lot of what they suggested we used to start the nonprofit later. For example, they wanted health services to be brought closer to them, which is something I had never realized. I just assumed that they were okay, but I didn't realize that the nearest health center was 20 miles away. And they don't have public transportation, so they would have to walk or carry the person in a stretcher. Also, they wanted to strengthen the groups of people—community volunteers who are trained to herd gorillas back when they come out, the HUGO Human and Gorilla Conflict Resolution teams, or Gorilla Guardians. They also wanted more health education, so it's not just a one-off activity, but a continuous event. And a lot of what they proposed is what we're doing in the nonprofit, actually.

So, the way that we're educating communities is through trying different methods. We've tried drama—theater groups, which worked well. You reach many people quickly, but you can't follow up on each of them to see how they're changing. But then we realized you also want behavior to change. So, we work with community health and conservation volunteers, and we teach them to do conservation work. Then, they go out to people's homes, and they carry out education either in the home or a group of people living in the village of perhaps 10 people. They talk about the benefits of being healthy, hygienic, and having the children you can manage, so you can look after them and not go to the forest to poach. Also, the dangers of eating bushmeat, because that can also make you sick, but also how people can make gorillas sick. This gives hope to change people. We currently now have about 429 volunteers who are reaching 10,000 homes, and they're getting to over 50,000 people in these homes.

So yes, it's very exciting. We're reaching more and more people. We call these community volunteers Village Health and Conservation Teams. The only thing we give them is incentives such as group livestock projects—group goats, group cows—and they go out and do the work of educating people about conservation and health. They're very happy, because they're more educated, and they're learning more than the rest. People look up to them in their community. Their leadership in the community has improved significantly.

Ashley: How does helping gorillas help the community? What's the connection between these two things?

Dr. Gladys Kalema-Zikusoka: When you help the gorillas and help them to survive, and they're healthy, then tourists come and pay money to see them, and a lot of that money is shared with the local communities. That's one way that it's helping communities. Many of the communities now have jobs just to be able to go to the National Park and monitor the gorillas. Local communities also set up accommodations like tents or cottages as lodging for tourists. Some of them are also able to sell food or crafts and take tourists on community walks. So, all of that helps the communities by protecting the gorillas. We also have a Gorilla Conservation Coffee social enterprise where we support local farmers to grow good coffee. Underneath every bag sold, money goes to support the gorillas and the work that we're doing to improve gorilla health, community health, and conservation education. When farmers get that extra money when they sell their coffee to us, we sell it to the tourists or outside Uganda—even in America—which in turn reduces their need to enter the forest to poach.

So, there are different ways that by helping gorillas, you also help the community. It's helping to lift them out of poverty and helping to improve their health. But also, when you help the gorillas, nonprofits like ours end up helping the communities as well. There are more NGO projects or non-profit projects because people want to support the gorillas, which in turn supports the local communities.

Ashley: How did COVID have an impact on gorillas? What was the work you did during COVID to study its spread and how that would affect the gorillas?

Dr. Gladys Kalema-Zikusoka: During COVID, the gorillas were impacted. Luckily, they didn't pick up COVID because of all the measures that were put in place, but COVID really changed things in some ways. Before you could just visit the gorillas without wearing a mask, but now you had to wear a mask because already we knew that gorillas were picking up common flu viruses from people at a low rate. COVID was a very big threat, as you saw. So, immediately we worked with the government—Uganda Wildlife Authority—to make sure all rangers put on masks, all tourists put on masks, and anyone going to see the gorillas puts on masks, and the Gorilla Guardians who herd them back to the park had to put on masks. And, when the local community members went out, everybody had to be sure that if they were going close to gorillas, they had to wear a mask because we were very concerned that they were going to get sick. The viewing distance between people and gorillas increased. It used to be seven meters; the government increased it to 10 meters. I know people often break the rules, but at least people don't get so close to them anymore, and they're wearing masks, and they have to hand sanitize before they go in the forest, which means that there's less disease entering the forest and less disruption to their behavior.

We were monitoring their health by collecting fecal samples from their nests. Every night, a gorilla builds a nest and defecates in it when they wake up before they leave their nest. You don't have to actually put a swab up a gorilla's nose to test them for COVID; you can test them from the fecal sample. So, we were able to see that they were not picking up COVID. But, we knew that the tests we were carrying out were sensitive, because in the San Diego Zoo Wildlife Animal Park, when the gorillas got COVID, they found out about it through fecal samples. So, we knew that these samples could be used to accurately detect COVID in gorillas. COVID had both a positive and a negative impact on the gorillas. The positive impact is that even after COVID, everyone will still have to put on a mask to visit them because the gorillas can get other respiratory diseases or a COVID variant. Everybody who goes close to the gorillas is now vaccinated: the rangers and the community members. So, that has really helped.

But during COVID, when there were no tourists coming because of lockdowns all over the world, the gorillas suffered a lot because poaching went up significantly. It went up because tourists were no longer providing money for people to buy food. People were desperate, and they were going into the forest to poach. A gorilla actually got speared by a poacher. He was not trying to eat the gorilla; he was hunting other animals like the small antelope, [the] duiker, and the bush pigs, and he set out for them. When he speared the bushpig, it screamed, and the gorilla charged the poacher to protect his family. The poacher then speared the gorilla out of self-defense, and that was really terrible. We started to get very concerned that if there are other hungry people like him, there are going to be more tragedies like that. So, the poacher got 11 years in jail for killing the gorilla, the duiker, and the bush pig, which is the longest someone has ever been put in jail for killing wildlife in Uganda. However, we were worried about other hungry people around the forest, so we started a project of distributing fast-growing seedlings called "Ready to Grow." It takes one to four months to grow. And when the seedlings grow, then people are able to have something to eat, and they don't enter the forest [to poach], so that really helped. That's something that we're continuing to do as part of our programs. We know that as long as you reduce the people's need to enter the forest to poach, then there is less negative interaction between people, gorillas, and other wildlife.

Ashley: Throughout your career, what were the main challenges you've experienced as a conservationist?

Dr. Gladys Kalema-Zikusoka: There have been a number, but the biggest challenges have been fundraising. When I started out as Uganda's first wildlife vet, no one had ever treated wild animals, so it was difficult to raise money for the vet unit at the Uganda Wildlife Authority because there wasn't a budget for it. Convincing people that it's important to give money to improve animal welfare, which in turn supports conservation, was important. I've been fundraising all my career. Then later on, people started to realize it's a good thing to do, because even when I left to do a zoological medicine residency in North Carolina Zoological Park and a Masters at North Carolina State University, the vet that replaced me had it a little easier because now they understood it was important, and they had a budget. He also managed to convince them to get more vets in.

But then after that, we started the non-profit, Conservation Through Public Health, where we were telling people human health is important in conservation. It was difficult to convince donors that we needed to improve human and animal health together and conservation and public health together. That wasn't how donors funded projects; they preferred to fund each sector separately. Fundraising has been one of the biggest challenges we've had. Now, some donors are realizing, if we don't address it together, we won't have long term outcomes. Other challenges have been treating animals—you don't just find them in a zoo or a clinic. They don't just say "I'm sick." Also, hiking to get to them is quite challenging, and even when you get to them, gorillas are very intelligent. If you want to get one animal in the group, you have to be aware of all the other animals in the family, as they could attack you. So, you have to be really careful about how you do it. That's a challenge in itself. But, we've learned how to work with biologists.

We learnt about gorilla behavior and various methods of handling: getting the other gorillas away and creating a barrier between the one that you're treating and the rest of the family. So that can be complicated. I've even been chased by elephants that were trying to get close enough to dart. I [ran] fast when the elephant came towards us. I always say that I [ran] faster than the men that day.

I think convincing people to protect wildlife is also a challenge, in a way, but if you show them that you also care about their health, they're more willing to listen to you.

Ashley: What are your next steps in your journey to conserve gorillas?

Dr. Gladys Kalema-Zikusoka: I would say that some of our next steps would be to expand the park because the space is getting too small for the gorillas. We're glad that the number of mountain gorillas [is] growing—we're very excited about that. But as you habituate more groups, they tend to spend more and more time outside the park because they have lost their fear of people. So, we would like to convince people to sell their land so we can expand the natural habitat for the gorillas, which is not as easy as it looks. Some people already said they're willing to do it, but it just has to be done in the right way. We also want to work in other countries in Africa that have gorillas and take our One Health Model that addresses the health of people, animals, and the environment together, to these countries. We started doing a little bit of work in the Democratic Republic of Congo. We would also like to share the model in other countries where there are no gorillas and [for] people to learn how we're carrying out the One Health approach, which is also good for savannah species and other kinds of species. But, we've decided that we're just going to mainly focus on expanding in places where gorillas are found.

In other areas where gorillas are not found, we're happy to teach and train others about our One Health Model so that they can also expand it wherever they are.

We're a small organization, and we can't have a lot of impact if we're going all over the place, and it's so hard to raise money to go everywhere. We're very happy to teach people what we're doing—we would love our model to spread all over the world, and one of the ways we can spread it all over the world is by training others to do it or influence other people to adopt it. It doesn't have to be exactly the same, but various aspects of what we're doing in the One Health Model can be adopted. This One Health Model is also addressing the climate crisis. Another example is with the coffee farming: when farmers plant shade trees that absorb carbon. Planting any kind of trees can help them with firewood, so they don't have to enter the forest to cut trees. Some of these things can help to address climate as well as biodiversity loss.

Ashley: How do you see climate change impacting conservation in the next however many years? Do you see any signs of climate destruction yet in your job?

Dr. Gladys Kalema-Zikusoka: We're seeing the seasons are changing: it's unpredictable whether it's going to rain or it's going to be dry. And the dry seasons are very dry, and the rainy seasons are very wet. If there's drought and then there's flooding, people's crops can get washed away. If animals are starving, people are starving, and people will turn to the forest, leading to negative interactions with wildlife. Maybe gorillas are going to go outside the park even more to look for foods that they don't find inside because the vegetation is changing, and therefore, they may get into more conflict with communities.

And then as far as disease goes, every time the temperature rises, there is an increase in infectious diseases, and the diseases stay around longer. Some of them are zoonotic, so they can jump between people and animals, which will affect the gorillas. For example, people at Bwindi never used to have malaria, because it's very cold for Uganda. But now people are beginning to get malaria. That's just one disease that hasn't affected the gorillas at Bwindi—it requires a mosquito biting a person and the same mosquito biting the gorilla. Other infectious diseases are also going to increase. So yes, the climate crisis is really affecting biodiversity conservation.

Ashley: Do you have a closing message to readers about the importance of conservation in the world? What does it do for people and animals, and why is it helpful?

Dr. Gladys Kalema-Zikusoka: I'd say that it's very important to protect the wildlife, because if we don't protect the wildlife—and by the wildlife, I mean the animals and the plants—we are going to end up destroying ourselves. Because when we protect the wildlife, we are able to benefit a lot more from the wildlife. By having trees and by having nature around, we're already having cleaner air, and we're having a healthier environment and water. But if we destroy the forest, and we destroy the wildlife, we end up destroying ourselves. The more that we poach and destroy the natural habitats, the more we expose ourselves to diseases that we wouldn't necessarily have had. We can end up killing all the wildlife till it goes extinct. We're so dependent on each other—the health and well-being of the people [and] the health of the animals and wildlife are interdependent. We have to make sure that we keep the health of our ecosystem and wildlife healthy, so that we remain healthy. Everything is interlinked. If we don't protect our planet, we end up destroying ourselves.

It's also important to engage women in conservation. It shouldn't just be about men. There should be engagement between women and men in everything, including conservation. It's also important to engage the children because they're going to be the ones who will be around to continue to protect the wildlife long after the adults have gone. They need to actually start to become the leaders of today and to lead the conservation efforts now, so that later on they will become even better leaders in conservation efforts.

Ashley: Did you, as a woman, face any challenges pertaining to gender in conservation or more generally speaking?

Dr. Gladys Kalema-Zikusoka: I'd say that most people don't expect women to go out there and work in remote places. They think it's a man's job to be in the wild and to go after the wildlife, to hold a gun. Sometimes people look at me rather strangely when I'm holding a dart gun, or when I'm walking into a bush with the guys. Now, I'm pleased that 20% of the rangers are women. When I started working with wildlife there were no female rangers. As more and more women are doing things like this, they realize, *Oh, it's possible to do this.* Then there is actually a difference. Conservation has been seen as a man's job, to go out in the bush and do all these tasks. So challenging society norms, even within my culture, it has been something I had to face. But I'm getting a lot of support now. A lot more women are now thinking of it as a career. There's an organization called WE Africa, Women for the Environment Africa, and I am a member of their Leadership Council. We are trying to mentor women to become leaders and realize their leadership potential in conservation. If you have an agency which is headed by women and engages women in conservation, they will understand the issues that women are facing and make sure that they're more comfortable working in the field.

Ashley: Is there anything else you want to add to your story?

Dr. Gladys Kalema-Zikusoka: Well, I want to encourage more and more women to write. I got to know Dr. Jane Goodall as a veterinary student, and I was inspired by her also because she started writing at a very early time in her career. I want to encourage more women to write about their conservation journeys, and I'm glad that I've written about mine. I am truly honored that Dr Jane Goodall wrote the foreword for my memoir, *Walking With Gorillas*. Hopefully, I will write more books. More people should write books, also, because there are very few conservation books written by women. We need many more.

What I learned from interviewing Dr. Gladys Kalema-Zikusoka

As climate change ravages communities and tears down the natural environments that have sustained us for so long, we neglect the respect we need to have for nature and the different aspects of our ecosystem. By ignoring our ecosystems' dire state, animals are starving and the impact on humans will follow, given that we are damaging the environment we inhabit. Once there is an acknowledgment of the consequences of exploiting the resources and animals that surround us, greater change can take place in terms of reducing global warming and saving future generations.

Dr. Gladys Kalema-Zikusoka's important and innovative work influences opinions in communities about the interaction between humans and wildlife and raises awareness of the interconnectedness between both: There is a balance in nature that humans shouldn't disrupt. I learned from Dr. Gladys Kalema-Zikusoka that the ongoing conflict between people and animals has created a loss in biodiversity, which future generations must address.

3

Jean Muenchrath

Jean Muenchrath is the author of the award-winning book *If I Live Until Morning*, which documents her experience skiing along the John Muir Trail and the tragic accident that followed on Mount Whitney. For five days, Jean was on a harrowing journey for survival, trekking through the wintry wilderness. Jean was born in Colorado and has always had a passion for connecting with nature and traveling. She worked as a park ranger for the National Park Service for over 30 years and also worked in Bhutan with the World Wildlife Fund.

Why did I want to interview Jean Muenchrath?

Jean's memoir stuck out to me because of her ability to bounce back, spread positivity, and give advice for coping with the trauma she faced. Especially with physical injuries, the recovery process can be long and grueling, causing those who go through it to sometimes suffer mentally. I knew that Jean was one of the rare people who was able to not only overcome the immense physical pain she had, but also turn her accident around to inspire others and donate her book's proceeds to charity. After facing a near death experience, I wanted to hear Jean's perspective on what her mindset was in that moment, and how she channeled this experience to follow her dreams and live life to the fullest.

Ashley: When did the idea come about to go hiking, and what is the John Muir Trail?

Jean: In the fall of 1979, I met a man in college named Ken who had just finished hiking the John Muir Trail a few months earlier that summer. The John Muir Trail is one of the most famous trails in the United States. It is the most scenic part of the greater Pacific Crest Trail, but instead of connecting Mexico all the way to Canada, the John Muir Trail is around 210 miles long. It goes from Yosemite National Park through the Sierra Nevada Mountains of California and ends on the summit of Mount Whitney, the highest point in the continental United States. Most people hike the trail, and a few people ski it. I had wanted to hike the John Muir Trail, yet I never really had the opportunity until meeting Ken. Ken later became my boyfriend and told me his dream was to ski the John Muir Trail.

I grew up in Colorado on skis, which piqued my interest in this ski trip. In many ways, cross-country skiing the John Muir Trail was similar to preparing for a mountaineering expedition—planning and training were absolutely crucial for success. Ken needed someone to go with, and I realized that it was going to be me. We trained together for many years to prepare for this journey. We ran, rode bicycles, and skied in the wilderness. I grew up downhill skiing, but in early adulthood I did more cross-country skiing and then more backcountry skiing.

Ashley: When did you start the journey? Were you nervous to go on the trip or were you excited about it?

Jean: We set out to ski the Jon Muir Trail in the spring of 1982. I was 22 years old at the time. I had a mix of nervousness and excitement. When I got about a third of the way into the trip, I had a gut feeling that told me something bad would happen on this expedition.

Ashley: So when the journey started, how was it going initially? Was it hard to go through it? Were there difficult conditions yet?

Jean: The trip started off fantastically. When I went on the trail, I don't think that many people had skied it before, maybe just a dozen in total. During the winter, both the trail and all trail signs are completely buried under snow. Back then, the only way to follow the general route of the trail was by using topographic maps and a compass. This was before GPS units and other portable navigational instruments. The terrain was extremely rugged. Over the course of our expedition, we skied, we gained 48,000 vertical feet, and descended 44,000 vertical feet. The landscape was beautiful, pristine wilderness—blanketed in snow with jagged rocky mountains. We skied a lot longer and further each day than we thought we would. We were making good progress for our trip.

That being said, we faced a lot of challenges. First, we had to delay our trip by one month due to avalanche conditions. This delay allowed the snowpack to settle and stabilize. There was also rotten snow that we had to get around. Sometimes while skiing, the snow would suddenly collapse beneath our skis, and we would sink in a giant hole up to our waists. Once the trip was underway, we still had to contend with one mountain slope after another that was covered in the debris left behind from earlier avalanches—broken trees, huge chunks of snow piled on top of each other, and limbs and branches scattered across the slopes. On top of that, we were on cross-country skis, which had no metal edges and were extremely narrow. The snow would sometimes be fluffy, and other times it would be hard crust which you could hardly turn your skis on. On the high passes, we also encountered waves of frozen snow, left from the wind, that were 6-18" high. These were very difficult to ski through. And we had to navigate to find ways to get safely across huge raging rivers, which meant being precise in our navigating to find mostly-buried (under snow) wooden bridges or go upstream to have a natural snow bridge that was solid enough to walk over to cross the rivers. We also had 14 high altitude passes, ranging from 10,000-13,000 feet, to cross. A few of them required technical climbing gear.

Ashley: Where did you sleep? Were there cabins along the way? How did that work?

Jean: We were self-sufficient on the trails, carrying everything we needed. Before the trip, we put food and fuel into 5-gallon plastic buckets and then skied them into the mountains and lashed them into a tree. This way, we had food stashed along the way once the ski trip began. Of course, we also had to later find the exact trees we had put our food in. We had a tent that we slept in every day, sleeping bags, mountaineering equipment, a week's worth of food at a time, and a camping stove—all of which we carried on our backs. I skied with 35 pounds in my backpack and Ken skied with 45 pounds on his back. The bulk of the journey, which we thought would last about a month, ended up being just over 3 weeks. At the end of our trip, our goal was to climb Mount Whitney, which was 14,505 feet high. We were going to end our trip that day and head home.

Ashley: At what point in the journey did the accident happen?

Jean: We began climbing Mount Whitney with our skis strapped onto our backpacks and reached the top. Suddenly, a huge lightning storm and blizzard came in. At this moment, we were seriously at risk of getting struck and killed by lightning because of our altitude. Our plan was to exit the mountains via the standard summer route, Trail Crest, but if we did that, then we would've gone straight into the storm for two miles and would be exposed to the storm for much longer. We decided to go down the North Face instead, which was more of a mountaineering route. We started climbing down the mountain with ice axes, which we could control our speed with. We were hanging on the mountain with our ice axes, backpacks still on, and our skis and poles strapped to the outside.

Not too far from the top of the mountain, Ken changed positions. Since the slope angle wasn't as steep as it was at the top edge of the peak, he went from hanging from his ice ax in the self-arrest position to a sitting glissade. He also thought it would be an easier position to be in while climbing down the mountain. He was now controlling his descent with his ice ax in this position. While I was still hanging overhead, he hit a patch of ice and flew 800 feet down the mountain.

At this point, I was hanging on my ice ax and could not see him. I did not know if he was dead or alive. I knew that I needed to get down the mountain as soon as possible to help him, but if I hurried, I would fall and die. I took my time going down to prevent making a mistake, which took several hours. Once I was at a place where I could finally look down and stand up, I saw Ken waving his arms. He came up to me and helped me down. When he came up from where he fell, he left his backpack, which had his rope inside. We brought a climbing rope with us for any sections of our ski trip where the terrain would require technical climbing skills to keep us safe during an ascent or descent of a dangerous slope. Our climbing rope was 160 feet long (standard length) and 7 millimeters thick. We also had crampons, carabiners, and snow and ice anchors with us to anchor the rope through. The storm continued and got worse. Ken, having fallen down, knew there were cliffs beneath us. We were 20 feet from getting to a ledge that could lead us away from and around the rocky cliffs below. Ken climbed down to the ledge to get his backpack and rope, which he had left at the base of the cliffs after his fall. With the rope, he could help me safely down the rocks to the exit ledge. It was getting darker and colder at this point. I decided to start down climbing rather than waiting for him to climb down and back up again.

Big mistake. I threw my skis down the mountain and was climbing down the rock with ski boots on. I got to a point where I couldn't go any further, as I couldn't reach any more holds in the rock, since I was shorter than Ken and didn't have access to the same holds he had used. I fell 160 feet, bouncing off the cliffs.

I fractured one place in my upper spine and most of my lower spine and right hip. My sacrum was broken in three places. I shattered my tailbone. I rotated my pelvis. I had nerve damage in my bladder and couldn't pee for five days. I had nerve damage in my left leg. I had a massive wound on my left buttock that turned into gangrene before I could get medical help. I also had a head injury and frostbite on my toes.

Ashley: Once you had all of these injuries, where did you go from there?

Jean: It took me five days from the fall to get to a hospital. When I got to the bottom of the cliff, Ken was down there, and he dragged me across the snow. Each time I tried to walk, I collapsed. He set up the tent on the mountain slope at 13,100 feet in the mountains. We laid in the tent for several days in a blizzard. The incident occurred back when there were no cell phones, GPS Units or Emergency Beacons, and no way to get help. We were also ahead of schedule, so no one was worried about us.

After two days and three nights being in the tent during the storm, we started to hike out. It took us two more days to hike out—we had to cover seven miles and lose 4,800 vertical feet without a clear trail. At this point, I was wearing 35 pounds on a broken back and pelvis to get out. If I left my equipment I would've died. For two days, while trying to get out alive, I sank through hip-deep snow in some places, while in other places, we also walked on hard packed snow, crossed back and forth over ice-clogged streams, and climbed down rocky ledges. When we reached a road where people would start their hike in the summer, we waited for cars to come by. There was virtually no traffic this time of year. The first car that came refused to take us to the hospital. The next car arrived with a young family and their belongings. Since they were taking a scenic side trip while moving across the country, they did not have room in their car for two injured adults and their backpacks. So, the father unpacked all their possessions and left them behind with his wife and baby in the parking lot. He was away for two hours while he rushed me and Ken to the hospital.

When I did get to the hospital in Lone Pine, California, it was more of a geriatric facility with two beds for emergency patients, meaning we—me and Ken—occupied both. Later, I was transferred to Scripps hospital in San Diego for another week. After that, I went home to my mom's house and was in bed for four months straight to let my fractures heal. I couldn't do anything for myself: I was a helpless adult in bed with a catheter in me to pee. My mother cared for me the whole summer. I was physically shattered. I still deal with the physical consequences today.

To get through this experience, I realized and applied the power of my mind and confronted the ultimate adversity of facing death; I had dreams and goals to give myself a sense of purpose, sought help, and owned my mistakes, and forgave myself.

When I was hanging on my ice ax and climbing down Mount Whitney, I first started to see how powerful my mind was. It was the most focused couple hours of my life. I was hanging off my ice ax which only penetrated a half an inch into the snow. If I tilted it wrong or lost my concentration, I would fall and die. I focused my mind. In my terrified, desperate state, I heard my inner coach speak up. My voice told me that I could do it. The voice in my head got me down to the point before I fell.

After my fall, when I woke up the next day in my tent, out of nowhere a mantra bubbled up from my gut. For two days, all I said in my mind was, *I'm going to live...* over and over. I set up this self-intention and perseverance in my mind.

Ashley: What happened next? What was your healing process like?

Jean: When I got to the hospital, doctors told me I would never be able to hike again. I lived to hike and ski. I again drew on the power of my mind—I knew I could prove them wrong if given time. Through the whole healing process, I had to use my mind to get through four months of nothingness.

Ken later became my husband and requested that I didn't tell people about my accident. I kept it a secret for decades. I noticed that keeping secrets held me back from processing things. I wound up having challenges with him since I couldn't cope. Our marriage eventually dissolved.

Ashley: Is there anything else you would like to add to the story in terms of the recovery process?

Jean: After this experience, I went to Asia repeatedly to see the mountains. Ultimately, it was the people and culture in Asia that shifted my perspective even further. I saw extreme poverty and suffering that is still hard for me to comprehend. When I looked, I saw people who had acceptance and an ability to cope. I didn't seem to find that as much in the United States.

This piqued my interest in eastern philosophy and meditation. I came back to the United States hungry to explore the power of coping with these things. I meditated and, with the help and support of Buddhist lamas, trained to make my mind stronger; I felt that I unlocked a tool that I could [use to] hone my ability to heal my trauma. I learned my mind could either be my best friend or enemy in terms of stress and, if I was able to control it, I could be in a better place.

In dealing with chronic pain—later in life, unfortunately, I got addicted to prescription pain killers that were for my injuries: morphine, fentanyl, hydrocodone. My doctor tried to get me off the pain medication, but his plan didn't work. I focused my mind on getting out of my addiction and went through a week of utter hell cold-turkey to get off these drugs. I built on the power I saw in my mind during my experience on Mount Whitney to help me time and time again.

I noticed that when I was really miserable, I only saw myself. If I could stop and think about what other people were dealing with, I realized my perspective shifted. Every time I have a challenge, I think back to Mount Whitney, knowing what I can overcome. I have turned my experience into a source of strength.

Ashley: When you were faced with death, what were you thinking – were you fearful of death?

Jean: Facing death made me question what it means to live and to die. Getting that close to dying gave me a newfound appreciation for life. When I was profusely bleeding all over the tent, I felt my life force leaving, a presence, a shadow of sorts over my body. I remember thinking *this is death*. Yet, I wasn't afraid. This was surprising to me, as every other time I have been close to death, like if I was on the freeway and almost hit a car, I would get a gut feeling of fear. But, at the moment when it was actually there and likely to happen, I didn't have any fear. I didn't want to die, but I felt peaceful. Whatever would happen would happen. I made a vow to myself: *If I live until morning, I will live my greatest dreams*, and then I went to sleep. This vow has served me for over 40 years. I have never forgotten it, and it informs my life.

When I was crawling my way out of the mountains, thinking I couldn't endure the pain of my injuries any longer, I would remember my vow and dreams. I had so much to live for: I visualized the Himalayan mountains as I walked. And I eventually fulfilled my dream. I made it to the Himalayas countless times.

When I was miserable in bed for four months at my mom's house recovering from the Mount Whitney injuries, I dreamed of a career as a park ranger. I trained and studied in bed to realize my dream. At the time, I had been working seasonally for the National Park Service (NPS). My primary job was working as an outdoor educator, leading nature walks, formal public programs, and evening campfire programs. I had to know a lot about everything in a given national park that I was working in—such as all about the plants, trees, wildlife, geology, history of the park, etc. Additionally, I had to learn and hone my communication skills specific to this type of educational programming. Later, I worked year-round with the NPS, which then had me overseeing other outdoor educators, training and coaching them, and operating and supervising visitor centers. Having a purpose that spurs us onward gives us a path through adversity. As life progressed, my greatest purpose, however, was not my career. Instead, it was my travels, outdoor recreation/adventure pursuits, and meditation retreats and studies in Buddhist philosophy.

Ashley: So, after the accident, it didn't discourage you at all from continuing to have the dream of climbing mountains and discovering new things? How did you conquer your past?

Jean: I went back to Mount Whitney, my life's enemy, 33 years later. I didn't know how I would respond. I found Ken's lost ski, and a heel of one of my ski boots, and I looked up at the cliffs. I screamed and bawled my eyes out. I was standing at the campsite where I should've died. The past and the present intertwined in a second. I realized I hadn't forgiven myself for down-climbing rather than waiting for Ken to grab the rope. I had to own my mistake. I still have to pay for it, but at 22 years old I did the best I could to stay alive. I believed there was a way out and didn't give up on it. What matters most is what we do with our challenges—rather than making myself miserable, I found a way to transform my life.

What I learned from interviewing Jean Muenchrath

Jean's story provides closure and support for those who have faced near-death experiences and for those afraid of death and the unknown. Her strong mentality and belief in her ability to get through her tragic accident and survive served as a moment of awakening rather than grief, fueling her drive to contribute her story to the world and demonstrate the level of self-awareness and maturity that was created as a result.

Near-death experiences also can, as was the case in Jean's story, create a newfound appreciation for life. When in the aftermath of such an experience, Jean felt determined to live life more fully, recognizing the parts of her life that are the most valuable and the true meaning of existence.

4

Leah Witman Moore

Leah Witman Moore is an author and public activist for inclusivity. Her memoir, *Loving You Big*, speaks of her path through parenthood and the challenges she faced. She teaches English and adaptive theater to high school students and has been a recipient of the Teacher of the Year Award, which is awarded to ten New York City teachers annually. She works to change the narrative regarding people with disabilities through sharing her personal experience as a mother of a daughter with cri du chat, a rare genetic disorder.

Why did I want to interview Leah Witman Moore?

Like many others, I believe that the narrative surrounding people with disabilities needs to change. It is disheartening that, in today's world, children and adults with disabilities are stared at, lack sufficient career opportunities, and therefore have trouble connecting with others. They seem to be people on the outside looking in, lacking some common human experiences that are vital to their happiness and growth. Leah's memoir, *Loving You Big*, shaped my perspective on what it means to have a disability and to be the parent of a child with a disability. It also opened my eyes to the ways in which we can deal with the unexpected realities life poses. I knew a conversation was needed.

Ashley: Could you introduce yourself to readers?

Leah: By day, I am a high school English teacher, and I also teach adaptive theater. I've been teaching for about 20 years now. I'm a mom of three. By night, I'm an author and a public speaker about inclusivity. I'm currently going back to school to get another degree. I'm from New Jersey and my husband's from Texas. We have lived in Westchester, NY for almost 18 years now. I'm currently working on some more books as well.

Ashley: When did you first find out your daughter had cri du chat? Could you walk me through the process of finding out about the diagnosis and understanding what it means to have a child with a disability?

Leah: My daughter, Jordan, was born in 2011. When she was about six months old, doctors realized she wasn't meeting any of her milestones. My husband and I started the process of early intervention to figure out what milestones and support she needed, and she went through a series of tests. By the time she was 18 months old, she was diagnosed with cri du chat, which is the deletion of the fifth chromosome. The doctor told us there was a chance she would never walk or talk and that early intervention would be the most beneficial thing for her. We had her enrolled in up to 20 hours of therapy a week, which included occupational therapy, physical therapy (PT), speech, applied behavior analysis (ABA) therapy, and feeding therapy. We tried to align her with all the doctors she would need. She got a geneticist and a developmental pediatrician. We found out when she was around four years old that she also had epilepsy.

Ashley: During this time period, what was your thought process once you did figure out her diagnosis?

Leah: Initially, I was devastated. I write a lot about the day of the diagnosis and what it felt like. A lot of the work I do now is helping to educate others about why my devastation was so intense. I was terrified. I didn't know if I would know how to be her mother. I was jealous of all the other babies I saw and all their parents who were able to go to the park and let their child play while I was still trying to figure out if Jordan understood me. I was mourning the life that I had anticipated her having: getting married or living independently. What I learned growing up in New Jersey is that despite the kindness and the education that was around me, society took kids with disabilities and put them on the outskirts where we didn't really see them. The messaging I got was that having a disability was something to mourn and hide. I had absorbed all of that, so when I was told that this would be my baby, I found nothing but sadness. I read a lot about trying to love the disability out of Jordan: with all of those therapies, all of that support, maybe we could "fix her." I've since learned that that's not the case at all. Life with her is certainly a challenge. She is not an easy cookie. But I find there's so much joy and so much of a new perspective of the way I approach the world, and I help other people approach the world. I have a better sense of what it means to have a child with a disability now.

Ashley: At the beginning of your book, you talk about your planned versus lived experiences. Could you expand on the ways you coped with the stress and challenges that came about in your life and what pathways you used to make yourself feel better in tough moments?

Leah: I think what's important about understanding stress and coping is that it's a cycle. The work is never done. The stresses of my everyday life have just continued. I've almost noticed I've had to relive them all. To cope, my number one priority is awareness of mental health. Everyone in my family has what we call a feelings teacher. For me, it is a therapist. My neurotypical child goes to see a group for kids whose siblings have disabilities. My two children with disabilities have that worked into their schedule. It's really important to process feelings and frustrations and manage our stress. I also believe in a creative outlet. I'm a writer and a singer, and I feel that it's really important to fight for that time so that my identity is beyond being a mother, a teacher, and an advocate. I also remember when I was a little girl before I had adult responsibilities and all these things taken away from me. I think it's important to know your social network and who you can rely on. When you're a family with disabilities, knowing that you don't always have to say "I'm sorry" and "thank you" for being in spaces is important. I shouldn't feel like I have to apologize for my children's disabilities. I never really know what's going to happen when we move into a room and we approach it with humor, but I can only be with people that do the same. I also am kind to my body. I remember that it's important to move around and exercise because I have to be really strong mentally and physically to take care of my children. The stress is immense and sometimes really isolating. I don't think a lot of people really know what our lives look like behind closed doors. I have to figure out a way to still go on dates with my husband, which is kind of impossible.

Ashley: What were some of the first microaggressions Jordan began experiencing? How old was Jordan when you first witnessed Jordan being discriminated against or experiencing microaggressions of sorts? What impact did this have on her?

Leah: I would say luckily or not luckily, Jordan is not aware of the world around her, which is stunning because she is pure joy. She looks in the mirror, and she thinks that there's a YouTube channel on the other side. She blows kisses at her friends and family. Jordan has moved through so many spaces totally unaware of the comments and the looks. One of the biggest microaggressions I witnessed that prompted me to be an advocate was at one of Jordan's dance recitals, but a bigger one that's happened since then is when Jordan attended summer camp. I was assured that the summer camp would be an appropriate place for her needs. And ultimately, she came home one day with her breasts exposed. I called the camp horrified. And they said, "Oh, we don't think she noticed." And I said, "But everybody else noticed. That's not treating her with any sense of dignity." I wondered who changed her and what situation she was in. It was one of these times where, because their answer was "Oh, well she doesn't know any better," that it felt like the fact that she was a developing 12-year-old girl didn't matter to them. I pulled her out of that camp, obviously, but it just really surprised me. It wasn't even a microaggression; it was macro.

Microaggressions are more subtle things like someone saying, "We don't have anyone who can work with kids like that here." Those are comments that I hear. Also, people making assumptions about her future, saying, "When you choose to institutionalize her, this will happen." I would respond by saying that is not the language we use, and those are not the decisions we're making. I would say those are some of the microaggressions I've experienced. The advocate in me now tries to educate others. There's this technique called "calling in" where instead of calling someone out for their implicit or explicit biases, you call them in. You would say, "So here's something you might not know about what's problematic about what you just said," or "Here's how this comment is making me feel, and I need you to understand why." I have to separate my emotion before I do that, but what's really beautiful about the technique is that you can do it a week later or a month later. It's still effective. So, in the incidence of the camp, I obviously pulled her out right away, but it took me quite a few weeks to be able to calmly explain what was so problematic, with my hope to create more systemic change for that program. With the people who've made some microaggressions, if it's someone that has any value to my life, I might try to educate them more, but if it's somebody just in passing, I usually just let it go and then make sure my kids understand why it is problematic. I will tell my boys, "That is not language we want to use," and, "This is why people think that."

Ashley: You talk a lot about the one-story approach to characterizing people who have disabilities. Could you explain a bit more about that and where people get discriminatory ideas from when characterizing those around them?

Leah: I'm citing the single story approach from Chimamanda Ngozi Adichie, who talks about it. We single-story people, and we make one story the only story. Historically, characters with disabilities have certain characteristics: a burden to society, a physical disadvantage like Captain Hook would have, not engaging in relationships, pitiable, laughable, a danger to themselves. There's a whole list of them. What's happened in media and in texts is that a significant amount of people get their understanding and development of what someone with a disability is like through the media, more than through personal interaction. I think it's 67%. If you've never met someone in real life who has a significant disability, and you're only getting it from the media, and then the media is perpetuating all of these antiquated norms and biases, it's really problematic. Within the last decade, even the last five years, we now see advertisements—Target for example may have someone in a wheelchair or with Down Syndrome—with disabilities integrated. Also, the person who is playing the person with a disability has one; they're not just pretending. But up until, I would say 10 years ago, we were getting the stories of *Of Mice and Men,* where we have to kill Lenny at the end because he has a disability and that's viewed as saving him. There's tons of examples of people with disabilities just being othered and separated. I'm hopeful that there's a change happening, but I still think there's a lot more that can be improved. I think sometimes the character with a disability is in a book because of their disability. For example, "Look how brave my little sister is because she has cri du chat," or they're used as a source of bullying, and they overcome it. So even *Wonder*, which is a gorgeous book, is still kind of problematic if you were to put it through an ableist lens. It's very nuanced, but one of the movements now is working towards different groups getting voiced authentically through characters.

Ashley: I know in your book you talk about how one of your sons also had a disability. Could you explain that a bit more?

Leah: I have two boys that are twins, the older one was born with excess fluid in his brain, and he has learning disabilities, sensory processing issues, attentional issues. Pretty much any sense processing disorder that exists, I think this munchkin has. He's now 8, and his name is Austin. He's at a much higher readiness than Jordan and is reading and writing, but he also has OT, PT, speech, a lot of dysregulations to his body, and he's in a co-taught classroom for that. We're still sort of navigating what his needs are. His twin brother has a rare blood disorder, which is even more updated from the book. So, we also now have a child with a medical condition. Each one of my babies now has something that they're handling beyond just growing up.

Ashley: Do you have any advice for coping, overcoming, and navigating being the parent of a child with a disability?

Leah: I think you, as a person, have to remember the person that you were before all of this started and remember how that person moved through hardship. I think what happens is the communities of people with disabilities give each other advice, rightfully so, so use your humor, or use your emotional response. What I'm noticing is nothing fits for everybody. There's this notion of self-care, especially for a woman, especially for caretakers. Design self-care that's authentic to what you actually need. There are some people who are going to get a manicure and take a walk and that is going to cut it. There are other people where that is not what their self-care looks like at all, but they're trying to fit into that self-care bubble. This can almost make you feel worse because you're like, "Well I won't feel better if I'm not doing X, Y, or Z." Ask yourself: *What does it look like for me to be in relationships in my life and build my support system?*

Ashley: You talk in your book about "Ladybug Warriors" (kind-hearted people who help and accept others) in society. As a society, what are some things you notice that people do that make you or your child feel more comfortable and accepted?

Leah: I think the number one thing is acknowledging we're in the room without making us feel othered. So smiling and saying "Hi, how are you? Do you need anything?" These are lovely social interactions between strangers. So, Jordan is now 12. She is so chatty and loves to listen to strangers and ask them questions. My favorite days are when people will just pause for a minute and listen to her. She'll want to know: Who was the president when you were born? Who's your celebrity crush? Do you have any siblings? A lot of strangers have paused what they're doing and responded. And we move on our way, but that fuels Jordan so much and maybe took 10 seconds of someone's life. You can tell within an instant the type of person someone's going to be when she like runs up to them. I think it's just those social norms of kindness, just smiling, and acknowledging I don't want to look pitied, and you don't have to feel sorry for me. Yes, I might need your help, but ask and I'll tell you what I need. That means the parent will say, "Oh, we're good. We're just kind of temper tantruming on the floor." Or, "I could use some help if you wouldn't mind." This would help with daily interactions. The next layer is *what stories* *are we taking in?* I love when people kind of vet their own social media feeds, and who have stories other than the lives they're living themselves. I think that then helps them to move through the world and create pathways for other people and amplify these voices. That's the way people can be more ladybug warriors societally, even if they don't have someone in their own lives to support.

Ashley: How are social interactions hard for children with disabilities? What are some things people can do to open themselves up and be more understanding?

   Leah: Yeah, this happens with the little ones. If we're talking about the little ones, it happens with modeling, and it happens with their parents. So when any of my children or even my own students are younger, little kids don't really care who they're playing with. So, they might say, "Why are they wearing those braces?" If the parent says, "Oh, it helps them walk," it's normalized, and we just move forward. But if the parent says, "Oh, I don't know, we shouldn't ask that, it makes them uncomfortable," then the kid senses that otherness. I think around middle school I start to observe what I call politely ignoring. No one is bullying. No one is making fun of somebody with a significant disability anymore. But there's not a true sense of inclusivity. That's because they're not really sure what that would look like. So, it's up to the kid or the teachers or the community leaders to find the connections. So, do you both love soccer? Do you both like makeup videos? Jordan right now wants to make makeup videos, which is actually age appropriate for 12-year-olds. Even if she can't play in the same way, she probably could have some really good times with other 12-year-olds right now. Some of my students are amazing artists. So, if they could sit next to another child who's drawing, it's redefining what interactions look like. I think the neurotypical kid finding that pathway of saying, "Oh, I also love this, let's do that a little bit together," or inviting people to sit at lunch, even if there's nothing to say. Just being near somebody can really help. It's the hardest piece. Because when it's not done well, the kids with disabilities can sort of become like a project. Not done well, it's like you get community service hours for hanging out with this child. But done well, it's just another really lovely interaction. My son said it really beautifully last week when he said, "Hanging out with Jordan is so fun because the world is just so happy and beautiful for her. When I walk around with her, I see how beautifully she sees the world." I was like, "Yeah that's gorgeous, right?" It's just another way of taking things in and everyone should have a chance to interact. Jordan does have a best friend. I think they mostly just stare at each other and throw dolls back and forth. I mean, they're so cute. They go to dance class together, they carpool places, and they go trick-or-treating together. She is able to have some of those relationships. She has a crush. She has a lot that's typical about her.

Ashley: So generally, do you think the fact that people are sometimes more reluctant to include someone with a disability makes it harder on the kid with the disability?

Leah: In neurotypical people's relationships, there's almost a little give and take of friendship-building. Based on the ability or the readiness level of a child who has an intellectual disability, it might not be a friendship in the same way. But to foster that relationship, I do think it has to come from a neurotypical kid listening to the cues from the child with a disability. So, for example, if you went to school with my daughter, and she kept gravitating towards you, and said, "I like your hair," you could easily say, "Oh, thanks" and walk away. Or you could say, "Oh, thank you, what's your name?" And then the next time you see her you could say "Oh, hi Jordan," and it starts to go a step further. Otherwise, you're going to get stuck in a rotating script, and it's up to the neurotypical student, probably, to help move away from the script. If we're talking about physical disabilities, that's not the same at all.

Ashley: Do you have a final message to society about being a parent of a child with a disability?

Leah: I would say that one of the things we use in teaching is called being a self-reflective practitioner. After you teach a lesson, you go back and think about what was successful about that lesson and what you would do differently. Not all parents have to be advocates and not all advocates have to be parents, but to do any of this work well, when you're on a path that you did not expect to be on, you have to be really kind to yourself and be reflective of what's working. That success is not going to look like everybody else's success. But if you're saying, "Oh, you know what, we did this thing successfully, and this worked really well for us, and this is what didn't go well"—in that state you feel motivated to try again. The number one thing is to remember that you do not have to do any of it by yourself. There are so many organizations and supports that are available and free and accessible that no one, regardless of any identity marker, would ever have to do this all by themselves. I think that's a huge message.

What I learned from interviewing Leah Witman Moore

Leah struck me as someone who has been successful at educating others on how we can prevent the exclusion and marginalization of people with disabilities by sharing the unique perspective someone with a mental disability has (in this case, her daughter, Jordan). To create a society where a disabled person can thrive, we each need to contribute to an environment filled with empathy and understanding. Especially in schools, children with disabilities may face deep isolation. What if instead of politely ignoring, we listened? What if by doing this we could create a new story in our minds for people with disabilities rather than sticking to the typical stereotypes we have used to associate with disabled people for so long? If each of us is just a bit more open-minded, this could be the start of something incredible. As Leah has taught me and many others, if we can reverse the stereotyping that goes on and shift our paradigm, perhaps some of the challenges people with disabilities face can be mitigated.

5

Dr. Kateryna Terletska

D r. Kateryna Terletska is a Doctor of Physics and Mathematics and the head of the Laboratory of Mathematical Sciences at the Junior Academy of Sciences of Ukraine. Dr. Terletska also works as an oceanographer, investigating extreme internal waves in oceans, and promotes science amongst younger generations. She was awarded the L'Oreal-UNESCO for Women in Science Award in 2019 and has a PhD in Physical and Mathematical Sciences.

Why did I want to interview Dr. Terletska?

Since war puts a halt to the everyday lives of its victims, education consistently seems to suffer. More students are fearful of going to school in chaos and must go to basements and shelters during attacks. This takes a toll on their education, and many people who are victims of war are suffering mentally, hindering their ability to learn and be productive. I was curious what a prominent scientist and educator like Dr. Terletska would have to say about how war impacted her work and what the current state of Ukraine is. Firsthand accounts from people suffering in a war provide a sense of emotional understanding amongst people looking to become more educated about war and its impacts.

Ashley: What is your background, and what was your childhood like?

Dr. Terletska: I was born in the Soviet Union. Growing up, I enjoyed solving problems and applying mathematics in everyday life. My dream was to understand how mathematics could describe the world around us, and I eventually achieved this dream when I helped with the Chernobyl Disaster. I joined the Department of Modeling Marine and River Systems to mathematically model the consequences of the Chernobyl accidents. After that, I again used mathematics to model the consequences of the Fukushima disaster in Japan (another nuclear accident). My field of interest is numerical modeling of internal waves. Internal waves propagate in the interior of the ocean. Such unseen waves can exist when water is stratified, that is, when it consists of layers of water having different densities. The South China Sea has the biggest internal waves in the world. Mixing caused by internal waves results in a vertical transport of water and heat throughout the ocean. Internal waves play an important role in distribution of heat within the climate system.

Ashley: What challenges have you faced from the war in Ukraine, and how have they impacted you?

Dr. Terletska: When the war in Ukraine hit, I couldn't believe something that bad could happen. One day, a Russian airplane was flying above us, and it fell down near our house, and there was a massive explosion. We were living in continuous explosions everywhere, hiding in basements. I thought about what would happen if Russian soldiers came to our house; eventually, my husband told me, "Please go away," and I said that I wanted to be with him. Later, I was shocked by how much violence the Russians were doing in the occupied territories. I realized that I made the right choice by taking the children away. I decided to go with my sons and supported a mission from the Austrian and German soldiers, which helped Ukrainians escape from Kiev from only one road in the south. No one knew German or English, so I was the only person who could translate what the soldiers were saying. Russian troops already cut off our other road to leave Ukraine. We just wanted to escape. We eventually reached Vienna, Austria.

In Austria, European institutions provided a lot of grants to support Ukrainian scientists. I currently have a position at Johannes Kepler University Linz. I have returned to Kiev several times to visit my husband and parents, but it is not safe, especially for my kids, because the last time we visited, there was an explosion nearby. It's very difficult to make a choice to stay or leave because lots of people are in Kiev, and my research team is in Kiev. I work from my department remotely at the Junior Academy of Sciences of Ukraine. Living in two countries is extremely hard. I am a scientist, but I am also a mom who just wants her kids to be safe. Education in Ukraine is not normal because, during attacks, kids keep going to basements and shelters, and sometimes decisions need to be made for remote studying. During emergencies, kids cannot do anything. If you hear rockets or drones all night, it is terrifying, and you cannot sleep and work effectively. There is a psychological impact: we are all really, really tired and not productive.

If the war lasts three–five years, I'm sure the world will still support Ukraine and its education. But mentally, people are exhausted and cannot perform as they should. Without a solution to the war, we will all die. We need to work with diplomacy to achieve our goals.

Ashley: What advice do you have for people in the Ukraine dealing with adversity? What is the current situation?

Dr. Terletska: The new generation understands that Ukraine is their land, and they want to be in Ukraine. I have a girl from my department who is 22. She wants to stay in Ukraine because she said, "It's my country. I'm not going to leave my country." I like this and want to make mathematical courses for Ukrainian kids who want to be here. I don't know what the situation in Ukraine will look like if our territory is divided. I worked in South Korea for ten years and know how it is. South Korea and North Korea are divided and have absolutely different lifestyles. Throughout all of this, I have had a family to support me, and I think for everyone it's important to have strong support. I hope Ukraine will not be divided, and I want to come back to my work in Ukraine with a newfound strength and willpower to move forward no matter how terrible the obstacles I face are.

What I learned from interviewing Dr. Terletska

Dr. Terletska's resilience and continued determination to promote science in Ukraine provides a source of strength and a voice behind the need for continued education and support for Ukraine. As Dr. Terletska said, the psychological impacts of war have made people exhausted mentally, and there is no clear fix to this problem. But once people's stories are spread, more and more people can resonate and feel less alone in their grief and pain associated with war and all of the far-spreading consequences it has.

6

❧

Emilie Béatrice Epaye

E milie Béatrice Epaye is a legislator and Member of the National Assembly of the Central African Republic, as well as a former Government Minister. In frequently challenging circumstances, Emilie has promoted safeguarding human rights within her own country for many years, and she is actively involved in the work of La Fondation la Voix du Coeur (The Voice of the Heart Foundation). This foundation mentors street children, providing a refuge from violence or abandonment for children where they are also provided with other basic nutritional, educational, and health needs. In 2015, Emilie won the U.S. State Department's International Women of Courage Award.

Why did I want to include Emilie Béatrice Epaye's story?

Emilie Béatrice Epaye has played a highly influential role in The Central African Republic, a country that doesn't always have enough attention brought to it in the media. The life-threatening attack Emilie survived and her effort to support marginalized groups demonstrates her lasting impact as a legislator and promoter of democracy in her country. As someone who influences parliament and actively works to break the cycles of violence her country faces, Emilie's story demonstrates a need for social justice and fighting for a better path for younger generations in areas facing violence.

Ashley: What is your background and what challenges have you faced?

Emilie: I have been confronted with several difficult situations in my life, but the event that I experienced on January 14, 2020, in the middle of the legislative election campaign which almost cost me my life, is the one that I chose as a difficult experience.

I am an independent Member of Parliament from civil society [and] an activist for human rights, the promotion of democracy, and the rule of law. My association, Fondation Voix du Cœur, is the first reference organization for the care, family, and social reintegration of street children and children in distress in Bangui, the capital of the C.A.R. and its surroundings.

I was elected four times as a deputy in the constituency of Markounda, a scene of rebels and armed groups in the northwest of the Central African Republic, bordering southern Chad. On December 12, 2020, the electoral campaign opened, and I confidently hit the road the next day to travel 445 kilometers to reach Markounda.

I had the assurance that the election security strategy put in place by the government in cooperation with MINUSCA following the APPR (the Khartoum Peace Agreement of January 2019) was going to work. In Markounda, I was welcomed at the entrance to the town by the population who accompanied me to my residence as they usually did. By the time I arrived and rested a little, I heard gunshots, and my house was surrounded. My campaign vehicle was taken away, another vehicle riddled with bullets, and my residence completely looted. My life was saved thanks to the intervention of MINUSCA Blue Helmets. Unlike my last visit to the region, the armed groups came together to create a Coalition, the CPC, to prohibit the organization of elections. I didn't know, because they had made the decision, and I wasn't informed. Even the press had not broadcast the news.

The elections were postponed.

On my return to Bangui, I decided not to give up, knowing I should win these elections at all costs. I am one of the rare people who could raise awareness and mediate between the armed groups to stop the hostilities between them and stop the violence against the populations. I am one of the rare people who could denounce the violence of armed groups against women and girls and who tried to document the facts each time in order to denounce them on a national level. I am also the person who raised awareness among traditional chiefs and other community leaders about social cohesion and living together. How could I let it all go?

I could only maintain my candidacy to be able to intervene at the national level as a deputy in order to be involved in decision-making for the search for peace and reconciliation of our people.

This is how, upon my return to Bangui after the attack, I decided to organize my electoral campaign remotely with women, young people, and certain traditional leaders through the telephone and WhatsApp because in Markounda the operator, Orange, has installed 3G.

And I won the elections in the first round among three candidates. I am currently using my position to demand the rights of incarcerated former child soldiers. Many have been released from prison and are undergoing training and reintegrated into their communities.

Others returned to school. With the help of partners, I was able to build a center for the promotion and protection of women, which is an essential place for the empowerment of women and which still needs support.

I continue to defend human rights, democracy, the rule of law and living together. Today, I am respected because of my commitment even if, with the decline of democracy, things become difficult.

What I learned from Emilie Béatrice Epaye

Emilie's fortitude in being elected demonstrates that courage and a drive to help protect your country or community from violence makes you a role model to society. By recognizing injustice and combating it at the risk of her own life, Emilie refused to give up because of her belief in democracy and human rights. Emilie made significant progress in protecting women in the Central African Republic, setting an example for all of us to have our voices heard, potentially becoming forces for political change. I hope we can also exhibit the kind of courage that Emilie has when faced with our own challenges in the future.

7

Colonel Kathryn Spletstoser

Kathryn Spletstoser, a retired United States Army Colonel, served 28 years in the United States Armed Forces. She is a national security expert and a decorated combat veteran who served four combat tours in Iraq and Afghanistan. She was also appointed by the U.S. President at the time, Former President George W. Bush, as a White House Fellow and has served as a Special Assistant at the Department of State. She held senior leadership positions at the Defense Counterintelligence and Security Agency, the Defense Threat Reduction Agency, and the United States Strategic Command. She holds a Doctorate in International Affairs and American Foreign Policy from the Johns Hopkins School of Advanced International Studies.

Why did I want to interview Colonel Kathryn Spletstoser?

Sexual harassment is an ongoing issue, and its far-reaching effects have been seen more than ever in recent years—especially since the start of the MeToo movement. When more and more stories are shared and more people speak up regarding their experiences, survivors of sexual assault can feel less isolated and addressing these issues can become more normalized. Colonel Spletstoser is an example of extraordinary courage and resilience in the face of assault. Despite the immense risks, her patience and determination in the face of adversity paid off—she reached a court settlement of nearly $1 million in her lawsuit.

Ashley: Can you describe your military career and any challenges that you initially faced?

Colonel Spletstoser: I was a career Army officer for 27 years. I started out after college after commissioning as a second lieutenant through ROTC and served for 27 and retired as a Colonel. I served around the world in peace and war with assignments in Germany, Korea, Afghanistan, Iraq, and Bosnia in command leadership and staff positions. I entered the Army in the second generation of women serving in the all-volunteer force at a time when more women were being integrated into the force and an increasing number of military occupational specialties were being opened to women. During that time frame, if you were a female in the military you had to work twice as hard and be twice as good to be competitive, successful, and excel. This is not an understatement, as many women in my peer groups can confirm. Women were not viewed as equally capable as men in being able to do their job, their ability to lead, or their resilience. It was a challenge, but with a lot of hard work I made it clear that I was a dedicated team player with mental and physical toughness and a strong work ethic, and I did quite well.

I didn't do it on my own. There were many great leaders in the Army I learned from and many who gave me a chance to excel. These included, mostly, great men who valued anyone who could meet the standards. Later, women were also role models. I had the privilege of serving as an aide to a female general officer, who later became the United States' first female 4-star general, that I learned a lot from. This illustrates that great things can happen when talent meets opportunity.

Deploying overseas in leadership roles, I was responsible for people in combat and had to make life and death decisions on engaging enemy combatants, protecting innocent people, and ordering troops into harm's way. I served in combat four different times, and each time was unique and different. Several big challenges I had to deal with as a leader in combat involved my time in Iraq. During my second tour there, a unit in my brigade suffered multiple casualties during an operation where four soldiers were blown up by an enemy improvised explosive device. Soldiers in my unit were tasked to assist in recovering the remains, and my unit then assumed control of future missions and roving patrol. Soldiers were scared because the missions were risky. As the second in command of the battalion assuming the mission, it was my responsibility to get soldiers ready to perform the missions, and I was going with them to lead by example and assume the same risks they were while trying to also ensure they had enough resources and firepower to engage the enemy. This bolstered their confidence, and we successfully executed that mission for nine months. I won't tell you that we didn't have casualties, because we did, but we also succeeded in performing the mission and succeeded against insurgents during the surge in Iraq. I have dozens of stories like this from Afghanistan and Iraq because that was simply a part of our day-to-day service in a war-time environment. Every single service member who was injured or killed made sacrifices that mattered for the nation, and we should always remember that.

Ashley: What obstacles did you encounter later on?

Colonel Spletstoser: After serving four combat deployments to Afghanistan and Iraq, I was selected to serve as a White House Fellow and as a Special Assistant at the Department of State, and later in my career I commanded the largest battalion in the U.S. Army and served in high profile strategist roles. Like anyone who serves and makes the military a career, I worked hard to progress in the military. Sexual harassment and misogyny were part of the experience along the way, which was never acceptable, but was often overlooked because there was little recourse, and reporting it often resulted in either retaliation, ostracization, or both. It wasn't until I was sexually assaulted as a Colonel late in my career that required me to report it, because I had a moral obligation to, given that the alleged perpetrator was a 4-star General nominated for promotion to the second highest position in the military. In this role I was concerned that he would have the opportunity to do this to someone else. I thought I was doing the right thing, and that because I also had a distinguished career that people would not only believe me but also take appropriate legal and administrative action against him to hold him accountable. I was clearly wrong. Senior leaders in the Pentagon and in Congress literally did the opposite. In my opinion, they closed ranks and set out to do whatever necessary to get him confirmed while also smearing my reputation and minimizing my service. I was once considered a rising star in my career, and then overnight, because I had the courage and strength to report a senior official for alleged sexual assault, I became a no one, a hated person, persona non grata. To have lost my reputation, friends, and colleagues and have people turn their back on me was mentally devastating and professionally destructive. People thought that my perpetrator was a good guy and didn't want to believe that I was telling the truth despite the evidence. The military decided not to prosecute him in the military justice system either, and he went on to get promoted and served for two more years.

Ashley: How did you feel having faced this?

Colonel Spletsoser: I learned the hard way that nothing prepares you to be exposed to the media when you have no help to deal with it. Even though I was offered the opportunity to stay in the Army, serve in future assignments, and compete for promotion, I decided to retire, because I knew I would always be viewed as tainted and labeled as a troublemaker. After I retired, I decided to take legal action and sued my perpetrator in federal court for sexual assault. The case set a precedent that opened the door for other victims and survivors of military sexual assault to seek equal justice under the law in federal court. When my case was ongoing and public, I found that being a public face for sexual assault in the military was very challenging. Yes, we succeeded in achieving a record settlement and a precedent was set, but it was traumatizing and mentally draining to go through. It took four years of fighting for my case in the federal court system. It ended well in my case, yet for most women and men who face similar situations, it doesn't end well. There is no justice, accountability, or closure. I hope the success I had in overcoming this massive obstacle can open the door further and help other people and deter service members from doing really bad things in the first place. Everyone should be treated with dignity and respect. You never really recover both emotionally and professionally when you go through the gauntlet of living through sexual assault and sexual harassment and how it is handled in the military.

Ashley: Is there anything you would say to women in the new generation about what you've learned from all this, and what we can take away?

Colonel Spletstoser: When you go through that type of adversity, it's a challenge to figure out how to live a productive life again and accept that life will not be perfect. I thought that positive publicity after our important case and settlement would result in helping to repair my reputation and in additional professional opportunities and that I could move on with my life. So far, none of that has happened. I'm hopeful that everything will get to a place that is worthwhile, but I know that it takes time. Like everyone else, I had hopes and dreams. My goal before all of this happened was to serve in executive roles in government, but the media exposure from the last four years has made that very difficult. No one wants to hire damaged goods, regardless of qualifications or merit. Somehow and someway, we need to change that paradigm. It isn't all bad, though. The past four years enabled me to recover from 30 years of non-stop, fast-paced military service and allowed me to reconnect with family and friends. I also had the chance to travel and complete my doctorate. I am one of the lucky ones I know as a military retiree and veteran. I know not everyone has this chance.

I would strongly encourage the future generation of women and military leaders to continue to fight to do what is right even when it is hard or seemingly impossible. Challenge bad decisions and laws, hold yourselves and others accountable, and stay positive and resilient in the face of adversity and challenges. Life is not fair or perfect, and it likely never will be. The goal is to keep trying to get there and help other people along the way.

What I learned from interviewing Colonel Spletstoser

Unfortunately, so many women who face sexual harassment are left with nothing but a tarnished reputation because they stood up for themselves. Interviewing Colonel Spletstoser shined a light on how such an experience can be overcome and how standing up for yourself despite unknown consequences proved to be successful. Kathryn's story, among many others, has served as a source of healing for women who are suffering because of similar workplace problems. Colonel Spletstoser's lawsuit was a milestone: it represented the first known settlement paid by the government for a sexual assault case against the U.S. military. Interviewing Colonel Spletstoser celebrates a huge marker of addressing sexual assault and achieving justice.

8

❦

Dr. Layla Salek

D r. Layla Salek is a behavioral psychologist who has used her own childhood trauma to write the memoir *Chaos in Color: A Memoir of Childhood Trauma and Forgiveness*. Her book paints a vivid picture of her familial trauma and her journey in overcoming it through forgiveness and mending her cycle of trauma. Dr. Salek also works to help children with mental illnesses and gives parents behavioral techniques to help their children.

Why did I want to interview Dr. Layla Salek?

Trauma's impact on mental health has always been a prevalent, ongoing issue that needs to be addressed. Now more than ever we are facing a mental health crisis, and although a lot of improvements have been made to our mental health system and the resources available to children in schools, more still needs to be done. I was interested in speaking with Dr. Salek because she has the experience of going through trauma and struggling with mental health as well as being on the other end of the issue as a behavioral psychologist who is using her traumatic experiences from childhood to help children who have mental health issues. Being someone who was able to use her own experience to better society and break a cycle of trauma within her own family, it became clear to me that Dr. Salek's story and work needed to be shared with more people.

Ashley: Can you tell me about your childhood and the adversity you faced?

Dr. Salek: I was raised by a single mom who was mentally ill and had untreated bipolar disorder. She was very young when she had me, only 19. It was almost like having a sister in some ways rather than having a mom. Most of the time she either left me with random strangers who I did not know or at home by myself for months at a time. When she would return, she would be overwhelmed with depression, not getting out of bed for months and then attempting suicide.

As an elementary school student left by myself at home with no food and nobody around me, I felt a deep loneliness. I ended up failing the 8th grade since no one was around to make sure that I went to school. It's terrifying when you have a mom who attempts suicide all the time. I had no idea if I was going to come home, and she was going to be dead.

I had no one else around me but my mother other than one family, the Melendys, who I was very close with and would go to. If I was with the Melendys, I always felt at home, safe, and comfortable. If I was with anyone else, I just wanted to be back at my house alone with my cat. The thing about being lonely and by yourself when you're little is that you get very used to that. Then you get around other people, and most people think you would like to socialize, but it feels very weird, as you are used to being alone. When I was younger, I would rather be at home than socialize. I would watch sitcoms on TV, and I felt like the families on the sitcoms were my own family. I could go to and listen to them and hang out with them.

During the long periods of time when I was by myself, I learned ways to adjust. I was poor, but most people around me were also poor. I had a relationship with God and learned to go to other levels when I was by myself. My best friend was my cat, Snuggles. I found that

I went to different places in my mind where I could survive and be okay. I didn't realize how much I could handle as a human until I went through all of this.

Ashley: How else did you cope with things going on in your life? Did being in school and away from home help at all?

Dr. Salek: School wasn't one of my ways to cope. I always was very intelligent and at the top of my class, meaning school was boring to me. I could finish assignments very quickly and was always the class clown. I went from being a straight A student to failing out—not because of not understanding, but because I was bored and didn't do my work.

Now in schools there is a counselor and psychological services on campus. You didn't have that when I was young. The teachers were sick of me. The coaches didn't want anything to do with me because I was failing out. I didn't have any mentors since there was no real mental health system in place to help me or help my mom. My classmates didn't know the depths of what I was dealing with. Even the Melendys knew my mom was bipolar, but they didn't know my full story.

Children have trouble coming forward and talking about their issues, which is why it is so important to have mental health services in school. There is always a reason children feel it is hard to come forward. We have more mental health problems today in Gen Z than in almost any other generation because of social media. There is a tendency of children not coming forward about a struggle until they are in their 30s, still struggling, and now with kids of their own.

Eventually, I was adopted when I was 15. The family I was adopted by remedied my failing, and I went to a private school. I was able to go off to college and then to get a master's degree at graduate school. Still, it is really hard for a family to adopt an older child. I found it difficult to go from being a child with my own rules to transitioning to structure and being a normal kid.

Currently, I go around and teach about mental illness, our mental health struggles, and forgiveness. I wrote about my struggles and became a psychologist: I wanted people dealing with mental illness to understand how they need support and the problems with our mental health system. Since I went into psychology, there would be moments when I would realize my mom is mentally ill and couldn't help the things she put me through. I knew my mother had a horrible childhood. Her mother's family is Native American, a group that suffers from mental illness and addiction at higher rates than any other group. She had no parents and grew up in the foster care system. My cousins, like my mom, are struggling with addiction and mental health illnesses. If you don't learn a different approach to life and take care of your trauma, you will raise your kids similarly, and she did. There would be moments and long periods of time when I felt very guilty that I didn't help more.

Ashley: How did you forgive your mom and move on?

Dr. Salek: My mom and I ended up reconnecting when I was in college for a bit, and I tried to get my mom help when I was in graduate school. I testified for her to get SSI, which is state funding for someone that can't go to work and has mental illness, and she got it. Forgiveness is ongoing. It's a journey, and you have to get to a place where you realize that hurt people hurt people. You must realize it really isn't about you, and they are hurting on the inside. I ended up getting married at 22, and we didn't talk after that. I couldn't have her around my husband and daughter because she wouldn't get help for her bipolar disorder. I created a life for my child where the trauma I experienced has never been a part of her existence. I look at things differently now. I see that the tendency of families is to push someone who is mentally ill away and then that person never gets help, making their suffering even worse, eventually making what they put on people in society worse. We have a whole society of people who need help, and it becomes separated from the ones that are trying to maintain their lives and be okay. At the end of my book, I wrote a poem, apologizing for trying to save myself, coming to terms with the guilt I was experiencing.

There was something in me at 15 where I knew I couldn't go through it anymore. I did not want to be in the cycle of trauma anymore, perpetuating the hurt I was experiencing. I had to save myself. I am the one in my family who stopped this cycle. I am the one who said no more. It is not easy to break generational trauma. I have always had an amazing relationship with God, the reason I spread a message of forgiveness. Hurt people hurt people. We need to support each other and talk about the mental illnesses people go through. Instead of pushing mentally ill people aside, we need to forgive and understand the underlying causes of their hurt. Nobody is out to hurt you, they just hurt on the inside.

What I learned from interviewing Dr. Salek

Dr. Salek's journey offers hope and connection to those grappling with trauma, inspiring them to embrace forgiveness and free themselves from the weight of their pain. Mental health is something that needs to be prioritized even more in society, and we need to find more solutions to combat the growth of mental illnesses. The first step in this is listening to other people's stories and reaching out if we think someone may be struggling.

9

Dr. Lise Deguire

Dr. Lise Deguire is an award-winning author who wrote the memoir *Flashback Girl: Lessons on Resilience From a Burn Survivor*, detailing how she survived a fire that nearly killed her in her early childhood. Her compelling story focuses on the isolation she felt as a burn survivor and how society viewed her differently as a child. Dr. Deguire uses her experience to inspire others and change the narrative surrounding how those with physical differences in society are viewed. Dr. Deguire also holds a doctorate in psychology.

Why did I want to interview Dr. Lise Deguire?

After watching Dr. Deguire's TEDx Talk "SCARRED Not Scary," I recognized more than ever the implicit biases present in society against people who look physically different. My eyes were opened to how the movie and entertainment industry uses differences to create one story for those with physical differences, typically painting them as a victim or villain. I knew a conversation with Dr. Deguire could offer insight into how a burn victim's life is defined by their self-perception and feelings towards themselves, which are, unfortunately, often influenced by society's views and treatment of disfigured people. If we continue to let negative stereotypes persist and view people with differences in a single light because of what we are subconsciously told, we may never truly be able to make disfigured individuals feel normal and accepted.

Ashley: Can you tell me a bit about the challenges you faced in your life?

Dr. Deguire: My life changed in an instant when I was 4 years old. I had a normal childhood with my parents and older brother until my family went on vacation to Lake Winnipesaukee in New Hampshire. It was our first night on vacation, and it was time for dinner. My mom was looking around the cabin for lighter fluid to start a barbecue. She thought she had found some, and I stood right next to her on the porch as she tried to start a fire. The fire didn't start. So, she took the lighter fluid again and poured it over the coals. Suddenly, there was an eruption that enveloped her and me. I was instantly burned on 2/3 of my body. My mother, who was also on fire, panicked. She realized that the way to save herself was to run through the fire and down into the lake, and she did. She saved herself that way but left me in the fire. Luckily, my father saw me in the ball of flame, and he was able to run around the fire and grab me from behind. He pulled me through the fence and threw me in the lake. He saved my life. But, at the end of that, my lower lip and chin were burned away, my arms were fused to my sides, and I was 3rd degree burned on 2/3 of my body.

Even now this would've been very dangerous, but in 1967 it was a miracle to live through what happened. I was taken to Mass General Hospital, which was the best hospital for burns at the time, and I had a brilliant surgeon who saved my life. I've had 75 operations and now laser treatments on my scars. I look a lot better, but I am still disfigured, and I always will be. I am still having surgeries to this day.

Ashley: After you went through the surgeries and the burns, did you feel like society viewed you any differently?

Dr. Deguire: After the incident, my life was impacted immensely. In school, other kids who didn't even know me stared at and bullied me. Back when I was a child, schools didn't really do anything about bullying. I was meant to be the one who took care of it. There was no help. Still, the kids in my school who did know me were nice, because I am friendly and get along with people easily. Although I missed a lot of school, the emotional and physical aspect of being a burn survivor was much harder to cope with. As I got older, there wasn't as much bullying and teasing, but it got harder in terms of dating. It seemed boys were not interested in me because I looked different. Even now, 50 years later, I am married and I am not getting teased, yet people stare. It feels terrible.

I still wind up in awkward conversations with people. People are nervous and don't know what to say. They probably don't want to say the wrong thing, so they end up avoiding me. It becomes up to the person who looks different to be the friendly one and start a conversation. Although this may not be an issue for me, as I am an extroverted person, for people who are naturally shy it is hard on them. Personally, I would like people to treat me normally, and then once I get to know them I would be able to open up about my experience.

Ashley: Do you think there's a root cause for this because children aren't exposed to differences enough? And they're too quick to judge people?

Dr. Deguire: The root cause of staring and bullying, I feel, is a lack of education and children not understanding that some people look different, but this isn't a reason to bully and tease them. Growing up, children are exposed to movies and TV shows with disfigured villains. There is Scar in the Lion King, a villain whose name implies his persona is derived from his difference. In Beauty and the Beast, when the prince is arrogant, he is turned ugly. When he finds love, he becomes handsome again, fitting our view of the hero of movies. Kids are taught from movies and TV shows to be scared of people who look different and to be prejudiced.

Research shows that people socially avoid people who look different and keep a distance from them. General inclusion would go a long way. Currently, I am trying to stop Hollywood from depicting scarred people as villains in movies. It is spreading prejudice and doing damage that needs to be stopped. Since only 1% of the population has a disfigurement, we tend to be overlooked. Still, I have found a growing community of burn survivors. The Phoenix Society for burn survivors provides support and education amongst us.

Ashley: If you had a message to give to burn survivors, or just people generally looking to become more educated on the topic, what would you say?

Dr. Deguire: My message to burn survivors is to persevere. Even the worst pain in the world eventually ends. I view burn survivors as heroes. I don't think they are people to be avoided or scared of. I think you can learn a lot from a person who has gone through that kind of experience: courage, compassion, and grace under terrible conditions. Instead of avoiding burn survivors, people should realize that they can find a wonderful person who looks different.

What I learned from interviewing Dr. Deguire

Dr. Deguire is someone who was able to take her devastating personal experience of being a burn survivor to better society and educate others on how we can make change. Sometimes even unintentional microaggressions, like staring at someone with a physical disability, can cause pain. Because it happens so often throughout the life of a person with a disability, it consistently puts the notion in their head that they're different, unable to fit into a rigid societal mold. Dr.

Deguire demonstrates that people with physical deformities simply want to be treated like everyone else. We need to dismiss false stereotypes in the media that promote one story when it comes to disfigured people.

10

Ulanda Mtamba

Ulanda Mtamba is an activist from Malawi and the Executive Director for GEM Organization. She also works as a Country Director of the nonprofit (AGE) in Africa. She advocates for the health and education of girls and women and works to prevent child marriage. In 2023, she was named one of BBC's 100 most influential women.

Why did I want to interview Ulanda Mtamba?

For so many girls and women worldwide, especially in more rural countries, they are told what their place in society is meant to be. They are often forced to get married as a child and give up on education. They are made fun of when they choose a different path. When this is ingrained into young women in society, it is incredibly hard to break this cycle. This is why when I came across Ulanda's story, I knew I had to speak with her. Not only did Ulanda break this harsh cycle in her own life despite immense challenges, but she also currently works on educating other girls and women on how they can as well. Her life-long mission is to educate those around her on girls' and women's capabilities and advocate for biomedical HIV prevention innovations.

Ashley: If you were just casually talking to someone about your career and what you do, how would you explain it?

Ulanda: I work for an organization called GEM that supports the equitable building of skills and access to opportunities for girls and young women through mentorship and coaching, leadership development, educational support, and social and behavior change interventions and services. But my story is cemented by the work I did for five years with AGE Africa. We advance girls' education in Africa and support adolescent girls and young women through scholarships. So we provide comprehensive scholarships to allow the younger women and girls to access quality education. In Malawi, we have challenges in terms of support for education. There's a higher percentage of adolescent young girls and young women, as you saw in the BBC documentary, who cannot access quality education and also those who drop out because maybe the parents might decide to marry them off, because they don't have the support. They feel like their children are just a burden, so they'll sell them off to older men to get married, or they'll just stop paying for any necessities, including access to education. The young people either go in the streets or find somebody who can marry them so that they can continue with their lives.

So, my work specifically revolves around supporting adolescent girls and young women to make sure they have access to education and provide the support that is needed most. Another thing that I do through this organization is the provision of life skills, because when we've been working as an organization in recruiting the support that we are providing, we noticed that because these are young people who are on the verge of exploring their lives and just want to know everything that is going on around their life, they didn't know much about setting their goals and knowing about sexual reproductive health and all that. So along the way, we noticed that, despite us providing scholarships, young people were still dropping out of school. They'll be pregnant, and they just decide to not go to school, despite [the fact that] we're paying all this. So, we commissioned this study, and we learned that a lot of young people in Malawi don't have access to information to know who they are, to have self-awareness, and to be able to set goals like "What is it that I want to achieve in the future?" and "Who am I?" and "How can I advocate for the issues that are affecting me?" For instance, if my parents are forcing me to get married, what is it that I can do? You know, children can advocate for themselves to say, "No, I don't want to. I want to continue my education and finish," and all that. We noticed all those elements: they don't know who they are, like the biological aspect of who they are. They didn't know that. So, the organization developed a curriculum, creating healthy approaches to success.

This curriculum was developed by young women in Malawi and other experts in different fields: gender, human rights, sexual reproductive health, and leadership. So, this curriculum helps to build agency for girls and young women and those who are in secondary school or high school. We build agency to make sure that they should know who they are and how they can develop their goals and be able to work hard so that they attain those goals. This program helped to identify, also, that girls need to make sure that they voice their concerns as advocates. We started building that agency within these young people. It helped our program to support the scholarships, and we've seen that with combining this program, young people are no longer dropping out of school. We see that our pass rates for secondary schools are around 98%, and almost 50% of our scholars transition to university, and those who make it to the university are graduating.

Much of my work is making sure that adolescent girls and young women have access to education and have access to information about sexual reproductive health, gender, [and] human life. Then I start building their agency and using them as advocates, because I always consider myself to be a really strong advocate, because I've gone through the same process as a young woman who grew up in a community where people were not really concerned with education, or if they're concerned, they might not just support the education. People are just dropping out, people are just being married off before they find themselves. So I had to stand up.

As young as I was, I knew that, for me, I wanted to go to school, I wanted to finish, and I wanted to have that independent life where you can make informed decisions and money later. So when I realized that I could access education, be better, get my degree, my master's degree, and now choose who I wanted to marry, how many kids I wanted to have, what type of a house I wanted, to which schools I want to send kids, I knew that education empowered me quite a lot. So, I started supporting a lot of young women also, but also not just in terms of education.

I call myself an advocate for adolescent girls and young women because I combined the issues of gender, human rights, and health education. I always say, as long as there are issues that are affecting adolescent girls and young women, I will go and advocate for them. I will fight tooth and nail until I get to the bottom of the problem or until I see young people moving in the right direction, then I'll be able to sit back and relax. Otherwise, if I can't be able to see that, I will stand with the young people and make sure that every time they see that there's a big sister there who is thinking about us, but also who is not just thinking for us but helping us to start voicing our concerns, to start building that agency to start being young advocates and stand up in conferences and meetings and say, "We want this as young people, and we don't want this in government," so communities should be able to listen. So those are the major aspects. We fight to make sure young people should have access to information on health, human rights, services, but also access to education, and, above all things, no young woman should be married off before the age of 18. So those are the major aspects of my work.

Ashley: Could you speak a little bit about what your childhood was like and when you began to see problems with the status quo for women in your community?

Ulanda: In the community that I grew up, which is a really rural area in Malawi, I had both my parents, and when I was going to school, I could see that there would be moments that if girls especially decided not to go to school, nobody was paying attention. You'll be in class, and you see your friends who are in your class, and you wonder where they even are, and nobody is concerned. And when they come back from school, and you ask, "Why did you not go to school?" they just go like, "Oh, it was my mom who told me to do this." Like, why? Young people will be sent for errands to sell like merchants, or they will just stay at home and nobody will pay attention to that.

Or they'll actually be taught that you should not go to school because you have to look after your siblings, or, if you're going somewhere, parents will ask if you can take care of the house. So, I grew up in a community where people were not concerned about a girl child. I could see these things when I was young and whatnot. And despite that, I had both parents always force me to go to school. And also because I had elder brothers and sisters who would always say, "We're going to school, all of us together." So I could really just join. But when you look at the community, it was not really so forceful about children going to school. Growing up, when I was proceeding with my school, I now saw that it became a mockery, because some people of your age are dropping out, and some are getting married, and you're still continuing going to school.

And you'll be mocked like, "Oh, you're growing up, you'll have kids too late," and, "You're just at that age that you need to get married, and you seem not to be concerned." The firstborn in our family, my sister, who now finished high school started working, and she was staying in another community where it was a little bit better; it was in the city. And she said, "You know what, you have to come over, you have to stop school on that side and come start learning on this side." So I was saved by that. My sister knew if I continued staying in my community, then I would not finish school because I would succumb to the peer pressure of my friends, and also the other parents and other communities because there were very few people who were going to school.

So, I moved in, and I went to this community where I now started being raised by my sister. That was so close to when I lost my dad. I lost my dad before I joined high school, which we called secondary schools. I was raised by her—her seeing me through primary school, finishing upper primary school, then going to secondary school. So, I was raised in this community, and it was much better, because people really were so much into education. The community was much better, but the school where I was going was very far, such that for girls to be walking and moving those distances was challenging. Oh my goodness, we faced quite a lot of things: being bullied, being beaten on the way as you were going or coming to school. People would snatch all your books or your food. So that was also challenging. The distance also was way too long. Maybe in the range of 10k, something like that. So, every time I would think about the distance, which was already another barrier. Every time you're thinking about the distance, you're thinking about this lapse. But to me, I was like, *No, no, no, no, no, I need to press on to see where it will end.* But this continued until when, as young as I was, I wrote to the national examination board seeking support, explaining that I needed a boarding school where I could be able to go to manage the issue of distance and to manage the issue of being bullied and all that. So, I got that space, and then I went to boarding school. I finished high school. I went on to go to the university and get my first degree. After I graduated, I started work.

Everything was okay. But I never got the satisfaction, like, *This is it.* I was like, *No, this is something that is still so huge.* I remember that my dad was somebody who also used to inspire me a lot. He used to tell me to make sure I get a PhD. He told me to make sure I worked so hard, "whether you be doctor or whether you be a professor," and then he died before I went to high school, but his words keep on coming back.

So, I was like, okay, after my first degree I need to do my master's degree, and in my master's degree I am currently planning to enroll for my PhD. I still listen to what my dad used to tell me. My journey was not easy. I had some struggles that I had to fight along the way.

Ashley: Can you expand on the ways you found to overcome these challenges and how you found it within yourself to keep fighting for your education?

Ulanda: So, what really was within me to start fighting was that I had young men who I could see. And within my class, I would also see young men who were doing well. So to me, it was that fight to say, "We're *not* different." Despite the fact that I'm a girl, it doesn't mean that even with all these challenges that I have to drop out. No, I can be like them; I can be like him. And whatever label that young men will reach, I knew I could also reach. So to me, it was that element of we are equal and nobody should be differentiating us just because of the gender aspect. No, because we could have the same interactions. We could do the same cause; we could both be bosses. He could be a boss; I could be a boss. So to me, it was that we are not different. So it's that that kept on keeping me fighting. We're no different from them.

Ashley: Do you have a message regarding the importance of educating women and keeping them in schools, given what you've seen in your country?

Ulanda: We win, trust me, we win. Because, just to give you an example, I've already educated more than five girls, and they're all graduates. Others are social workers, teachers, nurses. So, you can imagine just one person can manage to produce five graduates. It means, if we graduate, more girls can support other girls, and that's how we can change having uneducated women. And when young girls and young women are educated, we are better placed to sit on the decision-making tables and make decisions that affect us because we would no longer be expecting only a man to sit on a table to make decisions that affect us. If we're having problems with certain health care, certain interventions, it's us women who are feeling it, isn't it? So, we should not expect somebody to bring a solution for us for the issues that affect us. It should be us sitting on those tables, bringing in solutions that work for women.

Some young women are living with HIV; can we have some HIV prevention options that women should not be seeking support from men to use? We need more choices for young women to reduce the rate of new HIV infections. Women's bodies demand different health support at different ages of their lives. We are not like men, you know, so other things do not work for women—maybe they are tailor-made for men. We need to educate more women who can be our scientists to work on options that can be good choices for women. So to me, I always look into these aspects. If we educate more girls, more women, they'll be at decision-making tables, they'll be in Parliament to move bills that favor us, because if we give all this to men, they will shut down bills that affect us. To me, it's always that aspect. Let me give you an example. In Malawi, we had a readmission policy: when a girl was pregnant, they had to stay two years taking good care of their child, and they could go back to school after three years. We started asking ourselves as women, okay, for at least two years, where's the boy? What is the boy doing going back to school when you've kept a girl home for two years? Can we reduce this? Okay, what if this girl has got a very supporting family who can support the child as this girl is going to school? Then [can] we reduce it to one year or six months?

You see, so all these things only women who have been educated know, [and] they can start advocating for and understand that they can be able to start advocating to say no to two years, as there will be so much that this girl will lose. And most of the time, you'll find that these boys will be going to school, and they will start dating someone else. Or they go to the university, and they'll come back, and they don't want to marry this girl they impregnated a long time ago because they'll actually now say, no, you are uneducated. You see. So, it's all those elements that to me, I say, no, no, no, we give an education to girls and these young women will be empowered, [they] will be able to challenge some of these things that affect us, and we'll be able to support each other. Because other things were said when we were not on those tables. But if we're educated, we'll be able to demand that space, and be able to be present, and be able to move only the things that will be good for us as women.

Ashley: Have you seen significant change in the status of women from when you were a child to now?

Ulanda: There is so much that has changed from when I was young. Women, we couldn't talk and put in a say. You were not supposed to say anything. I'll give you an example: during menstruation. despite feeling pain, you're told not to say anything. You're taught not to take some painkillers. As a woman you need to endure the pain, how? You're taught not to say things that you should be able to. Why can't I take painkillers so that I feel better? You have to be strong, because you grow up and you'll be a woman. No, it's painful, and I should not be enduring that. Give me drugs, and I should feel better. Maybe, I can also go to school. But if you insist I have to endure, I'll be somewhere pretending I'm okay. But I'm not.

You see, so those were the things during our time. You move a little bit, you're in a marriage, and we were taught the same things: anything else that happens to you in your marriage, don't say anything. You'll be a disgrace, you'll be disgracing your family, so things like violence, you could not report. Even seeking a divorce was a tall order, but things are changing. Now, we are able to speak, and we are able to say, "You know what? When things are hard today, come back." You know, don't die in your marriages. We're able to conversate with our partners; we are able to say, "No, no, no, I have to go to work." We have moved some steps, good steps; we have made some strides. And if we continue, we will be able to start bringing this to an end. For instance, I always say if I'm at this level, my kids will not be like me. They'll be more vocal. There will be those who will demand more rights. They'll be able to say things that are right or wrong. For the reason being, we are able to say this is our agenda on the table and [are] able to embrace in the learning. My last born, she's 10 years old, and we're so different. She's able to challenge some of my decisions. She'll say, "No, no, mommy, that's not true." A long time ago, I would not challenge my mom. When you look at the girls who are making it to secondary schools and who are making it to the university, the numbers, not that there's a huge number, are much better than before, and those who are coming out as graduates, these [numbers] are much much better than before.

Ashley: What can future generations of women do to continue this advocacy and continue to institute change?

Ulanda: Future generations should trust in themselves, and they should take the challenge. They should not wait for someone else to bring about their rights. They have to work for it. They have to fight for it. Because nobody will say, "Come, we have this table here. Bring your agenda." They should create, seek for that space, and sit at those tables and carry their agenda with them. So to me, that's what I can demand of this young generation and the next generation. I say, "Nobody's going to do that for you." When I'm going out for meetings, presentations, if there is a young girl who is interested to be with me, I say let's go. You should be able to see what happens and voice opinions. Don't be shy. So for us now, who are already in the decision-making space, we need to make sure we're making deliberate efforts to create the space for the younger ones, just be there and keep on fighting and advocating. I'm in my 40s. My needs as somebody who is in their 40s and the needs of somebody who is in their 20s are different. I should bring on board those who are in their 20s to come and sit with me and share. It's affecting them, and they should speak their needs. What is it that is affecting them, and what change do they want to see?

Ashley: *Did you have anything else you want to add to your story?*

Ulanda: Believe in yourself. You know? My story is my story, and I believe in the power of my story. The more I tell my story, the more other women are empowered. So, let's keep on sharing our stories. Let's believe in ourselves, and what we can do. And let's believe that we have that power to bring change. It's on us to bring that change, and nobody else. This is the generation who can start: we should not wait for the next 100 years to come. Now, everyone at their own level can be able to bring that change. At each level, you have issues. Voice out and bring that change that is needed at that level. That's how we can move this movement.

When we were doing a documentary for the BBC, there was a report that indicated that it might take some 300 years to end child marriage. We were like, no, no, no, no. It means the younger generations are going to die and perish. Let's change this narrative now. In this generation, we don't want any child to get married before the age of 18. We cannot wait for the next 300 years.

What I learned from interviewing Ulanda Mtamba

Once more female role models like Ulanda can arise within our communities, more women become hopeful for a future that is defined by their *own* aspirations. The work of current reformers is not yet done. School drop-out rates for women due to arranged marriages and pregnancies will be lower. Girls will have the opportunity to explore their place in the world before it's chosen for them. This path continues to be carved, little by little. But as Ulanda said, "We cannot wait for the next three-hundred years." She and many other female advocates are working to change the narrative as quickly as possible, defying the impact perpetrated by generations of child marriage. Ulanda knows it cannot wait. She was once that girl who was made fun of on her way to school. She was once the girl who was mocked for not getting married as a child. But she stood firm in her beliefs. Now, she plans on enrolling for her PhD and continues helping other girls and women with their educational journeys—a story of resilience that can provide hope to those in similar situations.

11

Kim Phuc Phan Thi

Kim Phuc Phan Thi, also known as the Napalm Girl, is a survivor of a napalm attack during the Vietnam War in 1972. Nick Ut captured the horror Kim endured during the war in a Pulitzer Prize-winning photograph titled "The Terror of War." Kim currently works to symbolize hope and resilience for children in need through her founding of The KIM Foundation International. She is also a UNESCO Goodwill Ambassador.

Why did I want to interview Kim Phuc Phan Thi?

War and oppression are two things that remain stagnant in the world we live in. People go to war to fight and serve their country, and many come out of it with unresolved trauma or PTSD. And innocent bystanders like Kim are tangentially affected—they want no part in war, yet they're impacted significantly. When it comes to remembering the details and devastation caused by war, I find that photographs become ingrained in our collective memories. We attempt to connect in some way to a survivor's suffering through the vivid picture painted by a photograph. When I was researching the Vietnam War, I came across the picture of Kim titled "The Terror of War," which made me feel empathetic toward what she had gone through at such a young age. In an instant, a 9-year-old's whole life could unjustifiably change because of war. I knew that if given the opportunity to talk to Kim, whose resilience and forgiveness has allowed her to be a source of hope for other war victims, maybe myself and others could further understand the devastating impact of war.

Ashley: Could you tell me a little bit about the events leading up to the photograph of you taken during the Vietnam War? How did you grow up, and what was your childhood like?

Kim: My family was living in the village of Trang Bang. We were a wealthy family. My mom and my dad and my family ran our restaurant very well. My mom and my dad inherited a lot of land from my grandparents. We had a lot of animals and a field. Wow, we had a lot. So, I have a Great Uncle and he took care of all of this like a nanny, right? But more than a nanny, he took care of all of us and our animals and my mom and dad. Running a restaurant, we were so busy. I remember my family, my sister, my brother, and us growing up and going to school. For me, I just enjoyed life as a little girl. My favorite food is still guava, a tropical fruit. I just loved it, because we grew a lot of them, and they were so good. I still remember climbing on our tree and picking the biggest and best one that I would enjoy in the tree. My friend would come in and we would play around. That was so fun. I had a lot of fun playing with my friends and feeling free.

Even in Vietnam, they were having a war, but it felt far, far away. Not close to us yet. Then I learned that so many refugees came from another village, which was farther in the forest, to our village. And so my grandparents gave them a little land so they could build a little house, and each family could live together. I remember we had a big house with one part connected with a second part with the kitchen separated outside. And we had 100 acres, which my parents maintained. We had chickens, pigs, ducks, swans, and cats. I really enjoyed it. I just want to tell you that we had so much before the war.

After the war, we'd have less. We became officially poor. I didn't like it that way. When the Vietcong came over one night, they knocked on the back door. Normally before that, when they came at night, they knocked on the front door. Never on the back door, never. So my grandma and my mom and dad wondered, *Who is knocking on the door?* The Vietcong usually came and asked for supplies, but they never stayed. That day in June, they came with so many soldiers when they knocked on the door. My mom told me later, because at that time I was sleeping. When my mom opened the door, the soldiers told her they needed to stay in our house. My mom understood it was war. The Vietcong occupied my village, and they chose my house as the headquarters because it was big. My mom knew this situation was dangerous since we were in the house. So, she made the decision for us to move out. The only place we could go was the temple, because we thought the temple was a safe, holy place. My mom woke me up the day the Vietcong took over our house, and I remember I was so scared. I held her hands, and we moved into the temple with other village families that we knew. The South Vietnamese soldiers protected us in the temple. My house was completely occupied with the enemies at this point. When we stayed in the temple, I played with my cousins and brothers. We were not allowed to play far away; we were just allowed to play nearby the bomb shelter. I remember that. After I had lunch at the temple, I would play with my favorite cousin. His name was Danh and he was just 3 years old. We would chase black birds and have so much fun. We stayed in the temple for three days.

Then finally a color marker was dropped inside the temple area, indicating that the temple would be bombed. The South Vietnamese soldiers who had been hiding with us to protect us got very upset and told us to run out of the temple, because if we didn't we would die. The children ran the fastest. I ran with my brother and all the boys, but then I looked back at my 3 year old cousin who I loved, and I slowed down to stay with my cousin. One of the soldiers saw us running slower than the others, and so he picked up my cousin so we could move quicker. In that moment, we ran into the highway, and I saw these huge and fast airplanes with so much noise. I just looked up and saw them, and it startled me so much. They passed over my head, and I turned to look at them. I saw the four bombs right then and there. Oh my goodness. I saw the four black bombs landing down, and then I heard the noise, *pup pup, pup pup*. In that moment, I saw fire everywhere around me. It was right in the spot of the three of us—the soldier, my little cousin, and myself. I was wearing very light cotton, like little girl pajamas. The material of my clothes was not heavy like the soldier's. All my clothes just burnt up. I saw the fire on my body, especially on my left arm. That was just so scary. Of course, the soldier also got burned very badly, which I learned later. The soldier burned so badly that he couldn't hold my 3-year-old cousin, and he just threw him. My grandma ran up to them and saw my cousin. She picked him up and kept running. Journalists had been filming the whole thing. 10 years later, I was watching that clip, speechless, crying. I got burned very badly, but in that moment, I didn't feel any pain. But it was a big shock. I was so terrified.

Ashley: Do you remember any of your thoughts during the moment?

Kim: My thoughts were very sad. I thought, oh my goodness. Since I got burned like that, I thought I couldn't be normal anymore. I would be ugly, right? I wouldn't have normal skin. I wouldn't be normal anymore—people would see me in a different way. At that time, I remembered feeling this. But then I was so scared. I didn't see anybody around me, just the fire. I was scared and terrified of everything. I ran out of the fire, and as soon as I got out of the fire that was around me, I saw my two brothers, who were 5 and 8. I knew that they missed the fire, because they are boys, and they ran faster than me. Then, I saw my two cousins, a boy and a girl; they are brother and sister. Then, I saw some soldiers around there. At that moment, we keep running and running and running. During that time, all of us ran for a while. I remember I saw many people on the street who blocked it. I was so tired; it was hard to run anymore. I started and I stopped running. I remember one of the soldiers gave me some water to drink because I was crying out "Too hot, too hot!" They all had a canteen filled with water. The soldier pulled out his container, and then he gave me some water to drink. I still remember that. But then he wanted to help me, so he poured water over me, on my skin. That moment, after he poured water over me, I passed out. Later on, I learned that it wasn't a good idea to pour water over me because of its reaction with the napalm

I learned that there is a reaction of napalm with the oxygen in the water, which burns more with the water. When I look back on it, I cannot imagine if I still remained conscious, how much pain I endured. For that moment, I recount it as a miracle that I passed out, because I didn't feel any pain. I still remember that moment and many more.

Ashley: What difference do you feel your picture made in the Vietnam War? What message did it send across to people?

Kim: Even for myself, the picture made a big impact. I had a different feeling about the picture at the beginning, but then later it changed. Growing up, when I became a mother and got older, I learned from other people, as individuals, [that] the picture made a big impact in their life. Many, many years later, I met a lot of women and men who told me the picture had a big impact on them. It haunted them forever. As a little girl, the first time I saw my picture was at 10 years old. Fourteen months after I returned home from the hospital, my father gave the picture to me. He said, "This is your picture, Kim." And I'm like, what? Because I'm naked, just as a young girl, I thought it was ugly. And then I looked at my face. In general, when you take a picture, you usually have a funny face or make it beautiful, and it's a really good memory. But my picture was totally the opposite. I was crying, my body got burned, and I was naked and hopeless. I thought,

What an ugly picture. Why did they take that? I hated the picture. I didn't want to see it. It reminds me of that moment before I passed out. I had so many nightmares and so much trauma from everything I dealt with at an early age. I hated that picture. I hated it. And I didn't want to see it. But, unfortunately, my pain is my scar. It reminds me of where I came from. War is terrible. That is why the picture has such a big impact on me.

When I was 31, I got freedom in Canada, and I became a mother. The moment I held my first son, my first child, journalists found me in Toronto. The picture was brought up again to me. I had the picture with me then, because it was in the newspaper. So, the moment I looked at my child and held him, I looked at the picture. I looked at that picture for a while. Something changed. Something deep in my heart was moved the moment I looked at it. I did not want to let my child ever suffer like that. I knew, as a mother, I had to do something—to do my best to take care of my child, to protect him and not run away from the picture. I have to confess, when I had freedom in Canada, I just wanted to escape the picture. I wanted nobody to recognize me, because my dream was that when I had freedom, I could go to school, find a job, build my family, and have a normal life just like everyone else.

In 1995, when I was holding my toddler son, I was moved by an idea. I have to do a certain thing—I have to accept the picture. I have to go back and work with it because I don't want my child and all the children around the world to suffer like that little girl in the picture. In that moment, the picture became a powerful gift for me, which I didn't realize before. Being a mother was really a turning point for me. I considered the picture to be a source of power rather than a curse; I embraced it and no longer felt shame. Now I'm a grandma, and I take care of my grandchildren. I learned and am so thankful for learning the story from the photographer, who told me that, after taking the picture, he was so concerned that I would die soon. He took me to the hospital, and it feels like he saved my life. Wow, he became my hero.

And we still keep in touch, and I call him. He became a part of my family. We really respect each other and love each other like family.

Ashley: Could you speak about how you used your adversity to help others through your foundation?

Kim: During that time I stayed in the hospital, I looked at all the doctors and nurses around me. They helped me with their compassion when I needed them. They were there and helped me with everything. I enjoyed what was around me because everyone had something that made them end up in the hospital. I thought, *Okay, people are like me.* The doctors and nurses were inspiring me. I thought that when I grew up I wanted to become a doctor and help others like they had helped me.

I suffered a lot physically, but mentally I got a lot of help from people. I wanted to fulfill my dream; I wanted to keep my dream alive. My dream was to help others. I wanted to help others, because they helped me. They were my heroes, but I couldn't make my dream of becoming a doctor come true because of life circumstances. But one of my friends told me that there are so many different ways I could help others. Even though I could not be a doctor, I could establish a foundation which would help other child victims around the world. That is the way I kept my dream alive. From that point, the Kim Foundation was born. Our mission is focused on children of war. We want to help children facing violence and underprivileged children around the world. It is so difficult for me right now to see wars. I cry and cry and cry. I still remember myself as a little girl 52 years ago.

What I learned from interviewing Kim Phuc Phan Thi

One photograph can change the whole world's perspective simply by portraying raw human emotion for everyone to witness. Kim gave war victims a face, allowing them to no longer feel alone. Her story symbolizes one person's impact in changing our outlook on war and its consequences, a story that can promote peace and unity if it is spread to many others. In a world that is defined by cherry-picked images that can convey a false narrative, Kim's photograph sticks out because of the emotions and truth it carries. It is important to not let photographs as impactful as Kim's become diluted amongst the chaos that surrounds them. Kim's understanding of the photograph's necessity demonstrates the importance of being resilient despite pain and chaos. The photograph is also a reminder that feelings of sadness are just as valuable as those of joy. Its ability to evoke people's emotions and stir up indignance is incredibly important when fighting against war, as proven by the widespread attention that the photograph received.

12

Simone Dinnerstein

Simone Dinnerstein is an American classical pianist who has played with the New York Philharmonic Orchestra and the London Symphony Orchestra, as well as others. She has performed at Carnegie Hall and made thirteen albums, which all topped the Billboard charts. Simone has been nominated for a Grammy Award for the Best Classical Instrumental Solo. She also brought the Havana Lyceum Orchestra from Cuba to the US to perform eleven concerts. She is currently continuing to make transformative and original music.

Why did I want to interview Simone Dinnerstein?

Researching musicians, I found that in the musical world it is extremely difficult for musicians to do anything other than dedicate themselves fully to their career. Creating music and performing in concerts is so time-consuming and can be an immense source of stress, but this part of being a musician is rarely talked about. The amount of time and confidence needed to perform in front of huge audiences seems like it could be overwhelming, no matter how passionate a musician is. This is why when I researched Simone Dinnerstein, one of the most prominent classical pianists, I knew an interview with her would provide insight into balancing a time-demanding career with everything else in life.

Ashley: Do you want to start by explaining a bit about when your particular adversity started and how it came about?

Simone: Well, I've been thinking about it in a more general kind of way. Mainly thinking about the issue of being a professional and having children. Certainly, in the world of classical music, it's such a competitive field, and it takes so much time to work hard enough to be able to become a professional musician that it's really difficult to see how a child can fit into that lifestyle. I think that it also says something about our society in general, that children are such a gift for everyone, yet our society makes it feel like it's an individual's problem to deal with. And so as a result, it's really challenging to think about how you're going to be able to succeed professionally and have a child. In my case, I was very lucky in that I have a really great husband who helped juggle the challenges, but because of waiting for so long to try to establish myself in my field, it really made it so that I wasn't able to have more than one child, and I really wanted to have more. And so my particular adversity was that I went through lots of miscarriages after I had my son, several years later, when I felt that I was finally ready to take a break to have another child.

Ashley: So, what was the emotional impact of that? At what point did you feel that you were ready to have kids again? Why did you feel that you were ready at that point in your career?

Simone: Well, my career blossomed quite late. Classical music puts a great deal of emphasis on youth. Usually people who are successful become successful when they are in their late teens or early 20s. In my case, my career took off when I was about 34, which is quite late, and my son was 4 years old. So it really picked up at that point. I didn't feel that I could stop. I didn't think I could really take a break to have another child until my career evolved to the next level. And so I didn't start trying for another few years after that. And by that point, I was almost 40.

Ashley: In terms of your career and thinking about whether or not you wanted to have another kid, what ultimately made you wait? Did you feel that it would get in the way of your work? Or did you feel that maybe it wasn't the right time?

Simone: I didn't think that I had enough time to have another baby because I knew that I would want to take some time off. I was on this fast track of traveling for my career. I travel internationally to play concerts, and I have to practice many hours a day. It was kind of relentless, and it was already very difficult with just one child. Even though my husband was the person who was always at home with him—my husband is an elementary school teacher—it was hard. He was, fortunately, on the same schedule as our son, and that made things a lot easier. But even so, it was really challenging for me to manage trying to be a good mother while being in a different country for a concert. I think that I felt that I needed to become better at doing all the concerts that I was doing. Every concert that I played was a completely new experience. I wanted to have done several cycles of playing in this kind of way. I mean, it's a lot: there's a lot of stress involved in performing in large venues with prominent orchestras, and I was recording a new album every year. So, it was sort of like a relentless treadmill.

Ashley: How did you cope with that stress?

Simone: I didn't necessarily cope all that well; it was almost like I was on panic stations all the time. I was trying to just take one day at a time, and I really missed being with my son and my husband. And so I tried to be in contact with them a lot. I was multitasking all the time. I really felt like my brain never really switched off because I was either thinking about my music and about performing and the different anxieties associated with that, or thinking about traveling and all the challenges that were involved with that, or I was thinking about my family and trying to be as involved a mother as I could be in that situation. I didn't really have any particular way of coping with my stress, and I actually only have really started to process it. My son is now 22, living in London and pursuing a career as an actor.

Ashley: And how did you maintain your passion and your creativity during the time if so much was going on? How did you find ways to channel your creativity and connect more to music?

Simone: I find music endlessly interesting and exciting. I'm the type of person who really likes to create new collaborations, do interesting projects. I'm always thinking ahead. In terms of my career, in terms of my artistic life, I've always been very active. I don't have a shortage of ideas about what I want to do, and I also am quite a bit of a gambler. I always try to do something regardless of whether or not it seems like it's possible for it to have. For instance, back in 2017, I organized a concert tour in the United States with a fabulous orchestra from Havana, Cuba. It was a crazy thing to do, to bring 41 Cubans to the United States. But I did it: I raised all the money and booked all the concerts, and it was this huge, huge project. I think if you were at all a practical person, you'd think, *Don't do it.* So, I've always been the type of person who likes to do exciting and challenging things in my life.

Ashley: At what age did you start to develop your passion for music?

Simone: I started playing the piano when I was 7. It was because I wanted to, which I think is another slightly unusual thing, because a lot of my musician friends' parents started them. I requested this; I wanted to play the piano. As soon as I started playing the piano, I was just hooked immediately. I had a very romantic view of what it meant to be a concert pianist, which was partially based on movies that I had seen. And so, of course, my feelings about what it means to be a performer have changed a lot over the years. But it is a strange thing that I basically knew what I wanted to do from the age of 7.

Ashley: Circling back a little bit, you mentioned how you had some anxiety while performing. How did you overcome those fears? And did those fears go away over time? Or was it harder as you were performing at larger venues?

Simone: I've always struggled with performance anxiety, and I've tried many different ways of addressing it and have definitely become much better at managing it over the time. I've done a lot of self examination about the particular elements of performing that make me feel anxious, and a benefit of performing a lot is that it becomes less of an anxiety-producing problem.

Ashley: Do some of those fears go away as you start to play the piano?

Simone: It's really variable and slightly unpredictable because sometimes that happens; I will start performing, and immediately I just become fully absorbed in the music, and I no longer feel the consciousness of my nerves. And then other times it will just persist throughout the entire concert and be an utterly miserable experience. So, I think there are lots of elements at play. If I'm playing with an orchestra it can depend on how comfortable I feel with the conductor and the musicians that I'm playing with. Or sometimes it's worse if I feel jet-lagged. And then other times it's better because I've already performed in that city before, and so I feel more comfortable. It's a matter of being centered and focused. And whenever I have a difficult time, it's because I'm not able to think about what I'm doing—all I can think about is how I'm feeling.

Ashley: And how do you share your passion with your family and others?

Simone: My family have been really my biggest supporters, especially my husband. I've been with my husband since I was a teenager. And so he witnessed my whole process of studying to be a pianist and has really been with me every step of the way in my journey. I felt very conscious when my son was a child that I didn't want to force my music upon him. And I think that going to see concerts is very challenging for young people. And so he came when he wanted to, and it wasn't something that I tried to press on him. But now he really loves music, all different kinds of music, and he himself is a great musician. So I feel like my love for music, and my love for being an artist and leading that life, has definitely influenced him.

Ashley: How do you feel like you have grown and improved as a musician over the years? How do you feel like you've gotten to your milestones and achieved what you have?

Simone: I think through becoming more and more confident that I don't have to be like everyone else. My artistic sensibility is my own, and the more that I listen to my own voice as an artist, the happier I am and the better I am as a musician. When I try to second guess and be like what I've heard or be overly-influenced by the world around me, I feel that I have stopped listening to myself.

Ashley: Do you feel like that also kind of applies to your journey figuring out having kids and that role in your life?

Simone: It's hard not to think back and feel regret. I think that it's not helpful to feel regrets. Because when I look back at those eight or nine years that I waited after having my son, I was really busy, and I was really absorbed in my work. And I think that I probably needed to do that. But I also think that I felt pressure from the world around me; I felt that I knew I had to succeed now, or I was going to be too old. Maybe if I hadn't felt that way, I would have felt able to actually listen to my desire, which was to have another child. So now I've definitely accepted the fact that I only have one child whom I adore. But I just feel that as I've gotten older, it's definitely become clear to me that the only person that you're living your life for is yourself, and you have to make yourself feel fulfilled and happy, and it might not go according to a particular formula that you think you should follow.

Ashley: Do you feel that either way there would have been a sacrifice? Either you would have sacrificed a little bit of your career or you wouldn't be able to potentially have another kid?

Simone: Well, that's how I perceived it at the time. I'm not sure if that would have been the case. I mean, you never can tell. Perhaps I would have had another child and been able to take a break and been able to keep going in my career without there being a problem. But certainly, I think that if I'm going to look around me, if I look at other female pianists, very few of them have more than one child. And I can't help feeling that there's a reason for that. It's just really difficult to do. It was a very sad period of my life when I was trying for another child. And what I do regret is that I put myself and my family through that for so long.

Ashley: Do you have any advice to other women going through similar situations balancing a career and then balancing having children and raising children?

Simone: Well, I think that we should all try to make our society change so that we have more support. I also do try to advise young women, if they possibly can, to freeze their eggs. Other societies are much more supportive. I have a friend who's German, and in Germany, when women have children, they get I think at least a year of paid maternity leave, and even the men get that, too. It's a society that is saying that being with your child is actually an important thing, and we want everyone to be able to do that. We don't live in a world like that here in the United States. When you're in a job you get unpaid medical leave.

Ashley: So, if there wasn't as much of a burden financially and the government or jobs provided more support, do you feel like this may be a possible solution?

Simone: Support is very important and so is taking away the stigma of wanting to be able to spend time with children. Most of my female friends didn't take time off when they had children. They had nannies, or they sent their children to daycare. And the few that did take time off were extremely self-conscious about it and felt that they were somehow failing professionally. And I think that's really sad: it should be that everybody is able to spend time with their children without being judged as not being successful or not being ambitious.

Ashley: Is there anything else you want to add to your story?

Simone: I feel that as I'm getting older, I find that I focused on my career so hard for the past 30 years, and I think that it's possible to give yourself more space and room to enjoy your life and do other things as well. I've been somewhat monomaniacal in my approach to artistic life, and if I was talking to a young musician, I would say yes you have to work hard and practice hard and do all the things one has to do, but you also need to have friends and need to have relationships. I think that's really, really important.

What I learned from interviewing Simone Dinnerstein

As a woman, having a career while balancing having a child and thinking about the logistics of what that entails seems to be something that isn't talked about enough. Especially in careers that require a lot of time and travel, it can be hard to raise a child and feel like you have to keep up with your career—when, in fact, it is never wrong to take a break. Simone's perspective on the struggle of balancing a career and a family teaches us to strengthen our support systems and seek to implement societal change. If we have more laws in place allowing for more career flexibility and time off when women become pregnant, raising a family becomes less stressful and allows more options for women.

13

Cynthia Changyit Levin

Cynthia Changyit Levin is a mother, advocate, writer, and speaker. She is a widely recognized expert in teaching others the tools of effective engagement with key decision and policy makers and having a real and meaningful impact on social policies as a result. She wrote the book *From Changing Diapers to Changing the World: Why Moms Make Great Advocates,* which details her journey through parenthood and how it shaped her into an advocate. She works to combat global hunger and poverty and coaches volunteers on how to build relationships with members of Congress to have their voices heard.

Why did I want to interview Cynthia Changyit Levin?

Motherhood impacts the course of a woman's life in that new mothers must now balance having children with continuing to feel fulfilled and giving enough time to themselves. This is why, when I came across Cynthia's book, I knew interviewing her could help young women understand the challenges that come along with motherhood. Sometimes, mothers feel disoriented and alone and need to find social connections and relate to other mothers who are also experiencing motherhood for the first time. I was hopeful that interviewing Cynthia would address and spread more understanding of the challenges of motherhood.

Ashley: Can you describe your career, going into your childhood and how you grew up and how that shaped your future?

Cynthia: I am a mother, advocate, and writer. I grew up with my parents and sister in Moorhead, Minnesota. My dad passed away when I was 12, meaning I viewed my mom as a strong figure in raising two kids by herself. She was a registered nurse, and I watched her get her PhD as a child. She set an example, and I grew up thinking I would follow in her footsteps to get a PhD. In the 1980s, I saw her become the director of a county health department during the AIDS crisis. This specific moment of fear and uncertainty made me realize I wanted to do my part, too. Ways to get involved, like speaking to members of Congress or writing to newspapers, never occurred to me.

I still was unsure of what I wanted to do exiting high school. I went to college for engineering, and this quickly turned out not to be my life's passion. Despite my lack of passion, I was comfortable seeing myself as a project manager in corporate America and eventually got a job. I had the degrees but wasn't excited to show up at work. Once I realized this wasn't my life's purpose, I knew I had to set my life on a different path. A lot of people began to be laid off from my company. I saw an opportunity to be a stay-at-home mom.

Ashley: What were the struggles that you faced as a mom?

Cynthia: My first child was born in Chicago in December 2003, and this is when I began feeling isolated. Since it was winter, I was inside taking care of the baby most of the time. I began to settle into my new identity of being a mom and started to feel disoriented. I felt alone, since all my friends were at work, meaning I felt accustomed to being at home taking care of my baby without having another outlet to go to.

In the first days, I felt that I didn't know what I was doing. I tried nursing my baby for four days, and my baby was always crying. I watched my baby get weaker. I didn't realize the problem was that I had no milk, and my milk came in late for me: a week later. I called my doctor, explaining how my baby was never satiated, and the doctor told me my milk wasn't in yet, and my baby was starving. I had a master's degree in engineering, yet I couldn't solve this problem. I felt relief that the solution was so easy, but I also put myself down for not knowing the problem. I suddenly had a newfound empathy for moms who can't feed their children. My eyes opened to the problems other parents have, seeing my own limitations.

Ashley: In terms of advocacy, what prompted you to take action?

Cynthia: The things I loved to do, like volunteering, seemed to get sacrificed. I cared about the poverty I saw in my community, so I used to look forward to going to my local soup kitchen, but this wouldn't be an appropriate place to bring a baby. The winter months continued, and I started listening to the news, making me feel even more depressed. I noticed that my worst times were at night when I was alone with my thoughts. It seemed like I was hearing all the bad news in the world. I heard of an earthquake in Pakistan and a famine in Haiti, and I cried because I felt I couldn't do anything to help resolve these issues.

My husband quit his job to start a company, so I was also worried about finances and didn't have much money. A friend of mine at church reached out, having seen what I was going through. She invited me to write letters to an organization called Bread for the World. They had a yearly campaign about hunger and taught me how to write letters to Congress about global hunger. By then, I had another baby, and writing these letters and sending them off gave me a greater sense of purpose in the world. Still, as a mom, I felt at the bottom of my family's priority list. My baby and toddler needed my attention, and my husband was working, meaning his needs came next, since he was supporting the family.

I remember trying to take my baby and toddler to the children's museum. But since the toddler wanted to do active things and the baby wanted to rest, we all ended up crying. Everyone was overstimulated and not very happy. I didn't have childcare options that would work for us, given I had no family around me. I empathized with families working on minimum wage who didn't have childcare. When I had those low moments, I knew I could share my experiences to make the world a better place.

I decided to take the next step to not only write letters to Congress, but to write a letter to a newspaper editor about hunger. I got one of my letters into my neighborhood newspaper, which felt like a start. I kept writing and getting rejection letters from newspapers, and forty-two letters later, I got a letter to an editor of *The New York Times*. I wrote about how children who grow up in poverty have lower chances of succeeding in school and life in general, yet if we invest in early childhood, we can offer opportunities that were nonexistent before through the Global Poverty Act. I suddenly felt a greater sense of purpose in the world. Me, a mom sitting at home in yoga pants, could be part of the national conversation. I thought back to my mom working to combat the AIDS crisis and became proud that I too can be a part of public policy as well as be a mom. I felt worth something.

I started a blog and eventually wrote a book called *From Changing Diapers to Changing the World: Why Moms Make Great Advocates*, discussing my quest for advocacy and the struggles of becoming a mom. The tools to go and make change are present in the book to guide readers as they advocate. The one thing I feel I can teach people is to make their efforts concise and driven. I teach a format of writing and speaking effectively called "EPIC," standing for engage, problem, in-form, and call to action. By far, the most important form of advocacy is building a relationship with your member of Congress.

Ashley: Is there any specific tool that you think is the most important to know to be an advocate?

Cynthia: I encourage anyone who wants to do advocacy to join an advocacy group with a good reputation that is dedicated to being non-partisan. Poverty-based organizations do a great job of training their volunteers.

Motherhood is a hardship that is so common yet is rarely talked about because of the gender roles society is built on. I think it seemed easier to put aside my own needs because I had bought into these constraints myself. Currently, most of my work is in the space of child mortality and maternal health. My message to struggling mothers is to find fulfillment in life, whether through advocacy or a strong support network. You are not alone in your problems.

What I learned from interviewing Cynthia Changyit Levin

Once we normalize and spread awareness of mothers' everyday challenges, more and more people can feel less lonely in their struggles. Cynthia's insights on how to cope through establishing stronger social networks and becoming an advocate in your community makes for an inspiring story about overcoming challenges in motherhood. It was also interesting to hear about how she navigated growing her passion for advocacy and teaching others about how to get involved, sharing the rewarding feeling she experienced when she was able to help. Her voice was heard, allowing her to teach others how to advocate in their communities through the power of writing. This makes society feel motivated to delve deeper into passions, allowing people to be the best version of themselves.

14

Dr. Bernadette Lahai

Dr. Bernadette Lahai is a former Legislator in Sierra Leone and former Vice President of the Pan African Parliament. She grew up in a community and country where women have often been treated as second-class citizens when it comes to legal entitlements and protection through law. Dr. Lahai has made it her life goal to address women's entrenched status quo through successfully promoting the adoption of laws franchising women for the first time in several respects. She is currently the Minority Leader of Parliament in Sierra Leone.

Why did I want to interview Dr. Lahai?

In many countries, women are still treated as inferior to their male counterparts. Simply because of gender, women are subject to carrying out life paths already created for them, crushing their dreams and creativity in many instances. Dr. Lahai's determination to overcome historic obstacles ingrained in society is beyond impressive to me. Especially in education, there is a pattern of women being shunned for wanting a career. Therefore, Dr. Lahai's ability to not only fight for her education, but to also use her education to take legislative action to allow future generations of women to have more rights made it feel imperative to interview her.

Ashley: Could you explain what your childhood was like and your role as a woman in your community?

Dr. Lahai: I am from Sierra Leone. I grew up in a rural area and in a polygamous family. My father had several wives, and my siblings and I worked on the farm and lived together in our village. My father believed in education and spent whatever money he had to educate us. He chose to educate both the girls and boys in our household, despite us living in a male-dominated society. On weekends, my siblings and I helped out on the farm, since we lived in a rural area. When growing up in the rural area, I saw a lot of discrimination against women. Women lacked the ability to exercise rights in marriages. Women had limited property rights and low personal status. As a young child living in a patriarchal society, I felt appalled by the way women were treated and knew I didn't want to continue to live in a society which undermines female capabilities.

Ashley: What happened when you decided to further your education despite the stereotypes set in place for women in Sierra Leone?

Dr. Lahai: When I went to university, I was hopeful that I could further my education without being looked down upon because of my gender. Men still thought they were better than women. In an exclusive boys school, where I did sixth form, boys viewed girls as less qualified because you are a female, even though you worked hard and had achieved better scores in class exams than them. If you wanted respect, you had to be consistent and determined. I received my BA in Geography and Rural Sociology, an MSc Degree in Agriculture, and later specialized in gender issues in agricultural research in my PhD in Agricultural Extension and Rural Development in the University of Reading, UK.

Ashley: What did you do after this?

Dr. Lahai: I knew I wanted to combat this ongoing discrimination against women and girls. After university, I joined several women's organizations with a goal of working on educational access for girls and women to improve on their participation in nation building. I joined the Sierra Leone Association of University Women (SLAUW), myself being a beneficiary of the Geneva Association of University Women (GAUW) scholarship for both my undergraduate and postgraduate studies. I later joined the Forum for African Women Educationalists (FAWE) and the 50/50 Group, both working to train women and girls and build their self-esteem.

I was elected to Parliament in 2002 and stayed in Parliament for three terms of 15 years. I was the first woman in Sierra Leone to be the leader of a political party in Parliament. Sticking with my goal to improve the lives of women and girls, my major occupation in Parliament was advocating on behalf of women in rural and urban areas.

One of my biggest accomplishments was writing the first draft of the Gender Equality Law in 2011, which has since been amended and passed into law. This law, the Gender Equality and Women's Empowerment Act, 2022, seeks to provide a minimum of 30% of women in both elective and appointive positions in politics as well as improve women's access to credit, among other [things]. I also was a part of passing the Domestic Violence Act in 2007, which criminalizes violence in domestic settings. To address the property rights discrimination against women in my country, we also passed the Devolution of Estate Act, 2007, which allows women and children to be protected if their husbands died without a will. The Customary Marriage and Divorce Act, 2007, recognized traditional marriage as legal and official, just as Christian, Muslim and Civil marriages, and criminalized child marriage.

Ashley: Do you have a final message to readers?

Dr. Lahai: I gained respect from people because of my focus and diligence when it comes to my work. Going through a male-dominated society in Sierra Leone, I used this to motivate myself to institute change. In Sierra Leone, there were 124 members of Parliament and only 19 were women in 2002. Although it is hard to juggle between having a family and profession, I find it rewarding to be a part of a movement to change people's perceptions on women's rights, roles, responsibilities, and contributions in society.

What I learned from interviewing Dr. Lahai

Living through first-hand injustices did not stop, but rather motivated Dr. Lahai to challenge unacceptable social roles and customs by reforming the legislative framework in her country. She worked towards fundamental change in a system that had continuously looked past the issue of women being treated unequally and women not being granted the same privileges as men. Dr. Lahai's legislative work has been influential, and she sets an example for women looking to get involved in government and have a voice in their country in order to institute lasting change. Dr. Lahai's account of her journey to become educated and make significant changes in her country was inspiring to me, and I believe it can provide hope to women suffering in similar situations involving patriarchal societies by demonstrating that there is a way out.

15

Emily Rivers

E mily Rivers is a survivor of spiritual abuse and has published a personal memoir, *The Courage to Leave: A Memoir of Escaping and Moving Forward From Spiritual Abuse*, detailing how she gradually overcame her traumatic experiences in a cult to find the strength to form her own identity. Emily's story provides a source of hope to others experiencing spiritual abuse. She works to bring attention to important societal issues and is an advocate for those overcoming spiritual abuse.

Why did I want to include Emily Rivers' story?

When I first started listening to survivors of cults stories, I questioned where this corruption could have originated from and how someone could gain enough power to influence and exploit an entire community. It's devastating how so many cult survivors had been brainwashed beyond belief and had their entire life influenced by something they would come to realize was an abusive, destructive force. When I encountered Emily's memoir in particular, I realized the extent to which her life was altered and how much she suffered because of a false ideology that was continuously being fed to her. She had been forced to conform to this ideology because of everyone else around her, despite her doubts and slow realization of the wrongdoings that were unfolding. Something that stood out to me the most about her story was the lack of essential medical care in her community, even in life or death scenarios. This highlighted the power of the pastor's manipulation in being able to convert people's logical ways of thinking through threats. I knew I needed to include Emily's story for readers to experience a firsthand account of the experience of being in a cult from someone on the inside who is seeking to spread awareness to prevent future harm.

Ashley: What is a challenging experience you have faced, and how did overcoming it make you stronger?

Emily: As a child growing up in the Appalachian Mountains and in the Bible Belt, my life took an unexpected turn at the age of six. A car accident, which seemed like just a stroke of bad luck, became the catalyst for a series of events that would shape the course of my life. In the aftermath of the accident, seeking solace and answers, my mother turned to a church that promised community and faith. Instead, we found ourselves entangled in a high control, spiritually abusive environment that would test my resilience in ways I never imagined.

The church, which should have been a sanctuary, became a place of silent battles. For fifteen years, I grew up under the weight of rigid doctrines and relentless pressure to conform. Less than a year after joining this new church, my mother banned television, mandated dresses over pants despite the harsh Appalachian winters, and stopped wearing makeup. I was mocked for always wearing dresses, which was particularly embarrassing during sports when my skirt would fly up. Our attendance at services every Wednesday, Saturday, and twice on Sunday was compulsory; missing a service was equated with prioritizing ourselves over God.

The pastor ruled with manipulation and fear, delivering sermons in a shout and indirectly chastising congregants. His word was considered divine, and dissent was met with threats of divine or pastoral retribution. To question him was to question God, and that would send you to hell. Medical care was discouraged in favor of prayer, leading to tragic outcomes such as my mother's cousin succumbing to treatable skin cancer. She had constant pain and bleeding for years, finally losing half her face. The cancer ate into her brain and killed her.

The pastor's doctrine was confusing, emphasizing predestination and the need for divine intervention to achieve salvation. He said that God didn't hear just anyone's prayers. Parishioners were encouraged to "seek the Holy Spirit," an intense and exhausting process that involved physically tapping us under the chin and giving verbal prompts to speak in tongues—a supposed sign of salvation which I never experienced.

We were expected to dance in the aisles, run around the church, scream, and whatever else he could think of. If we didn't, the pastor told us we weren't saved, we were on our way to hell, and that the spirit of God was not in us. The pastor exerted control over all aspects of life, dictating acceptable media, reading material, and activities. The church forbade beach visits due to modesty concerns. To wear shorts or a bathing suit was to cause men to lust. If that happened, God was under no obligation to protect us from whatever happened as a result. Women were severely restricted in their roles and appearance, not being allowed to wear pants, makeup, jewelry, or to cut their hair. They were not allowed to preach or teach except to teach children and other women. Neither were women allowed to speak in church but were supposed to depend on husbands to tell them what to do and think. Men also faced strict grooming standards, not being allowed to have beards or long hair. Only the King James Bible was permitted. The pastor's manipulative tactics included threats to leave the church, which we equated to abandonment by God, coercing compliance and financial contributions.

When I was about 8, this oppressive environment led to my withdrawal from speaking to adults. I started to pull out my eyelashes and eyebrows and developed severe anxiety. I wished I had died in the car accident when I was 6. I harbored a deep wish to have never existed, and the strain of the church's influence irreparably damaged my once-close relationship with my grandmother.

The constant scrutiny and the fear of divine retribution took a heavy toll, manifesting as anxiety, depression, and eventually complex PTSD (cPTSD). Like many who have endured spiritual abuse, the scars were deep, affecting my view of self-worth, my ability to trust, and my concept of faith.

Amidst the years spent within the confines of a high control church, I endured an experience that would test my spirit to its core. When I was older, I worked at a factory with my pastor's son, who had stopped attending his father's church but later returned. During our time working together, he started making sexually explicit comments to me, which I found very uncomfortable. Despite my objections, his behavior escalated to physical harassment. One night, I retaliated, and he reacted violently, shoving me so hard that I had to run backward for about ten feet, trying to regain my balance. He came toward me again, shoved me again, and threatened me with further harm. Consequently, I left the job to escape the situation. Years later, while I was employed at a bank, he came into my office. At that time, he was engaged to a woman from another branch of the bank and warned me not to reveal his past actions to her.

In the aftermath of the assault, the community that I had been a part of, the congregation that should have been a source of support, turned a blind eye. No one took my side. My voice was stifled, my pain ignored, and my trauma was trivialized. The church's leadership, including my pastor, chose to protect their own, dismissing my pain and pleas for justice. This betrayal was a profound violation of trust, exacerbating the anxiety, depression, and cPTSD that had already taken root from years of spiritual manipulation.

Carrying the burden of what happened in silence, I grappled with feelings of isolation and shame. The disbelief and inaction of those around me made it all the more difficult to come to terms with the violation I had suffered. It was a stark reminder that sometimes the institutions and individuals we are taught to trust can be the sources of our deepest wounds.

For years, I tried to handle all of this on my own. I believed that if I could just be strong enough, faithful enough, or resilient enough, I could overcome the pain and the nightmares of the past. But healing is not a solitary journey, nor is it a sign of weakness to reach out for help. Coming to this realization was a pivotal moment for me. Reaching out for professional help was the turning point in my personal revolution. It was an act of reclaiming my narrative and taking back control. Therapy was the key that unlocked my prison of silence, allowing me to process the trauma, to understand it, and to grow beyond it.

The decision to seek professional help was not made lightly. It came with the acknowledgment that the trauma I faced was not a journey to carry alone. Therapy provided me with the tools to navigate the complexities of cPTSD. It gave me a safe place to deconstruct and challenge the harmful teachings I had internalized and to rebuild my sense of self outside the confines of the church's control. The support of therapists and counselors was a lifeline, helping me to navigate the complex emotions and trauma that came with being assaulted and then silenced. They equipped me with strategies to cope with the aftermath and to rebuild my sense of safety.

Through this journey, I discovered the paradoxical strength that lies in vulnerability. Acknowledging my hurt and seeking help did not make me weaker; it made me immeasurably stronger. With each session, with every moment of introspection, I was weaving a new chapter—one where I was no longer a victim, but a survivor, an advocate, a beacon of hope.

Despite the deep-seated fear and the risk of further ostracization, I found the courage to speak out. Breaking the silence was not just an act of defiance against those who had wronged me; it was a crucial step in my healing process. It was a declaration that my voice mattered, even when it shook, and that my story deserved to be heard.

Overcoming this challenge has not been a linear path. There have been setbacks and moments of doubt. The path to reclaiming my life was fraught with challenges, but each obstacle surmounted has only made me more resilient. I've learned that my experiences do not define me; rather, my response to them does. By seeking justice and speaking my truth, I've begun to rewrite the narrative of my life, turning a history of victimization into a future of empowerment. Each step forward has been a testament to my strength and resilience. I've learned to embrace vulnerability as courage, to see my sensitivity as a gift, and to find strength in my capacity to heal.

Today, I stand firm in my identity. The journey through the darkness has brought me to a place of light, where I can advocate for others who may be walking a similar path. I have transformed my pain into purpose, channeling my experiences into helping those who struggle with the aftermath of spiritual abuse.

The journey through sexual harassment, physical assault, and spiritual abuse has been harrowing, yet through it all, I've emerged with a newfound strength and purpose. It has made me more compassionate, understanding, and determined to be a beacon of hope for others. It has instilled in me a resolve to support others who have faced similar adversities. My story is only one of countless others, a narrative that speaks of resilience in the face of adversity and the power of reclaiming one's life. I want to contribute to a world where such violations are met not with silence, but with unwavering solidarity and action.

My story is a message to all who have suffered in silence: you are not alone, and with support and determination, you can overcome the shadows of your past and step into the light of a hopeful tomorrow. If my story can inspire one person to seek the help they need or to feel less alone in their struggle, then every step of this arduous journey will have been worth it.

What I learned from Emily Rivers

Emily's story made me become further immersed in the detrimental nature of spiritual abuse and manipulation and how religion, something meant to provide hope and clarity, can be used as an instrument for destruction if manipulated by power-hungry people. Emily, along with many other spiritual abuse survivors' stories, gives people struggling through manipulation in their faith a source of hope in combating and working past a period of life that was overshadowed by destructive individuals looking to brainwash and gain control.

16

❦

Jodee Blanco

J odee Blanco is a survivor of bullying whose story led to a movement
to institute change in schools across the country. Through her anti-
bullying program, "It's NOT Just Joking Around (INJJA)™", thousands of teachers and students have learned to approach bullying in
compassionate and productive ways. Jodee Blanco is the first survivor
of school bullying to pen a *New York Times* bestselling memoir from
the perspective of an adult looking back and trying to make sense of
their painful past. That memoir, *Please Stop Laughing at Me...*, is now a
seminal classic, and the work she does in schools has helped to fuel the
anti-bullying movement.

Why did I want to interview Jodee Blanco?

The first time I witnessed a hateful act at my school was last year.
It was during first period in English class, and suddenly, an announce-
ment came onto the loudspeaker. The principal told us a swastika had
been drawn onto the leg of a classroom desk. Everyone was angry that
one person could represent our school this way. More incidents followed. Transphobic messages were discovered written across a classroom desk and on a bathroom wall. We talked about it in class but
didn't know what to do. Could it be peer pressure from friends? Act-

ing out for attention? I knew after this experience that a conversation with an expert could help more people understand why bullying and hateful acts happen and how to approach this. When I came across Jodee Blanco, I knew I had found the perfect person to talk to. I wanted myself and others to hear a firsthand account of the effects bullying has on an individual. Hearing more stories will allow people to have more empathy and take more initiative as bystanders. Stories give a voice to students who were or are being bullied and allow us to understand the psychological impact of bullying and hateful acts.

Ashley: Could you start by introducing yourself and your story?

Jodee: Sure. From fifth grade through high school, I was the kid who didn't fit in. I struggled like so many other kids today, simply because I was different. My school years were unspeakably lonely and hard. I never imagined I would turn that pain into purpose. When I wrote *Please Stop Laughing at Me...* and it became a bestseller, kids from across the country started calling and writing to me asking for help. Some were as young as fourth grade and were threatening suicide. I gave up my career in the entertainment industry and started responding to these cries for help one child, one school at a time.

This is the genesis of my activism. I wanted to turn my pain into purpose. I've been working in the American school system now for the last twenty-plus years. I've done my INJJA program in hundreds of schools.

Ashley: Could you walk me through the thought process and emotions of someone going through bullying?

Jodee: I'm often asked by kids after I give a student presentation, "What was the worst thing that ever happened to you, and what hurt the most?" and my answer always surprises everyone. It isn't the friendship I was denied. It wasn't even the bullying itself, the teasing, or the exclusion. It was all the friendship and love I had to give that nobody wanted and they kept throwing back in my face. After a while, it accumulated in my system like a toxin and poisoned my spirit. For me, the loneliness was unbearable.

The other question parents and teachers ask me all the time is how to determine when bullying is beginning to have a long-term impact on a child. It's when that child starts asking, "What's wrong with me?" Self-doubt seeds the long-term effects.

Ashley: What are some of the hardest things you endured when you were in school?

Jodee: My archnemesis, a girl who had been rough on me all through middle and high school, invited me to a party. I was so excited; I spent all day getting ready. When I got to the address she gave me, it wasn't anyone's home. It was a parking lot in a forest preserve. All the cool kids came out, some of whom I deeply admired, and said, "Like we would ever invite you to anything." They laughed and high-fived each other and left me there while they went to the real party.

At the beginning of high school, initially a girl let me sit at her table with her and her friends on one condition: I couldn't speak to any of the girls at the table. One day she said, "You can't sit here anymore." I didn't know quite what to do. She stood behind me, and she flicked my chair. I fell onto the floor. Everybody in the lunchroom started to laugh. I stood up, and I walked from table to table, asking if I could sit down. There were empty chairs at every single table. But not one person at one table would let me sit. I ran out of the lunchroom, into the bathroom, and wept. If any adult in that school would've gone up to the kids in the lunchroom and asked what they had done to me, they would've all said the same thing. They would've said that they didn't do anything, and they would've been telling the truth. They didn't do anything. And that's exactly the point. Bullying, I tell students, isn't just the mean things we do. It's all of the kind things we don't do but know deep inside that we should. Things like letting someone walk to class alone or knowing that a certain class-mate would give anything for your acceptance, but instead of giving that classmate a chance, you judge and look down on them.

Ashley: Why may bystanders be reluctant to step in? Do you think students are influenced by their peers in a way that would promote bullying?

Jodee: First, we have to look at who the bully is and who the target is. The bully isn't a bad kid. The bully is almost always a child in pain acting out in a cry for help. There are two types of popular kids in a school: the elite leader and the elite tormenter. The elite leader is the caring, kind, popular kid. The elite tormenter is the popular kid who will create a lot of gossip and drama. What normally motivates the elite tormentor is pain, a lack of control.

The reason why bystanders are reluctant is fear. They are afraid if they stand up, they will be isolated or bullied, too. I ask kids when I give presentations in schools, "How many of you thought that if some-one bullied you in school it was because the person or people doing it didn't like you?" I tell them this is a myth. If someone is mean to you at school, it is rarely if ever personal. It is not because the bully hates you. Something else is going on in that kid's life that is making them afraid and angry, and they bring all those negative emotions to school, and they act out in a cry for help.

Decades later, the night of my school reunion, I found out the girl who set me up for the party was mean to a lot of kids that semester. That was the same semester her dad died. Her mother didn't get her the emotional support she needed. She didn't set me up because she hated me; she missed her dad and was scared and confused.

A classmate in seventh grade got a bunch of his friends to jump me in the school parking lot in a snowstorm and pummel me with snow. They also tickled me so that my mouth would open, and then had a contest of who could throw the most snow in my mouth. When

I started to cry because I was scared, they ran off, laughing and giggling.

My parents were furious and insisted that I tell the principal. I learned at my school reunion that this boy was going through things that semester I couldn't even imagine. His mother had abandoned the family several months earlier, leaving my classmate and his six younger siblings. The father descended into depression and began neglecting the children. Every day, this kid who had bullied me was sneaking food from the school cafeteria to feed his younger brothers and sisters.

After the incident with the snow, my family pushed the principal into suspending this student for a week, no questions asked. When he came back from serving his suspension, he was rail thin. When he lost that extra food source, what little food there was at home he gave to his siblings, and he just went without.

How I wish I could go back and handle those situations differently. I am not saying that if a kid is going through hell, it gives them the right to bully or be cruel to another kid. But what I am saying is that if we understand that, it can make forgiveness a lot easier. Also, I tell adults that traditional punishment doesn't work. We need to find compassionate, restorative forms of discipline that allow the bully to access their empathy and develop it like a muscle.

A lot of my former bullies are my friends now, and they are in my life. In fact, the girl who set me up for that party was the maid of honor at my wedding. Forgiveness is really important. I travel around the country and talk about forgiveness. I shift the cultural paradigm in the schools that I visit.

Ashley: *In terms of bullying prevention, what are some resources children experiencing trauma or hardship could use to stop them from turning to bullying?*

Jodee: There are different types of bullying. The overtly-bullied child is bullied in all the obvious ways. The invisible student isn't necessarily intentionally excluded or targeted. He/she is simply the child who isn't on anyone's social radar. Both types of bullied students face loneliness and humiliation.

Prevention begins with compassion.

For example, instead of suspending a student, have them perform random acts of kindness or come up with a creative idea for contributing their energy to an important issue or cause. The key is for that child to experience the impact of doing something that lifts others up instead of tearing them down.

We also need to teach kids how to tell, self-advocate, and advocate for others. One of the things I do when I work in schools is give students the tools to be able to do this effectively. I also train teachers and parents on how to support those ongoing efforts.

Ashley: Do you have a message to anyone being impacted by bullying?

Jodee: My advice to parents with a child struggling with exclusion or bullying is to find them a new social outlet, completely separate from school. Start by checking the local library or the chamber of commerce to find activities for kids. I encourage parents to meet the parents of other children engaged in the activity and coordinate a new social nucleus for their child one neighborhood away from where they live. This will provide them with social confidence and give them something to look forward to on lonely days at school. It will also give the parents and the school the time they need to deal with the bullies compassionately.

If you're a teacher or principal, implement compassionate forms of discipline that allow the bullies to access their empathy and develop it like a muscle.

And if you're a student struggling to fit in, remain true to yourself. And work with your parents or a teacher to find that new social outlet where you can make new friends and enjoy a fun activity. Local libraries and park districts are a great place to start.

What I learned from interviewing Jodee Blanco

Jodee's ability to reconcile with her past bullies and empathize with their situations really struck me. I truly believe forgiveness and looking into where hateful behavior comes from is a good starting point in confronting bullying. Through my conversation with Jodee, I learned that bullying is rarely personal. The bully is almost always someone in pain acting out in a cry for help, and that they need compassionate forms of discipline, not just punishment, which Jodee says often makes things worse. Jodee's insightfulness has been a guiding light for me in understanding and combating the issue of bullying, as I know it has been for many others, and I hope her message is spread to as many people as possible.

If you'd like more information on Jodee or to contact her, please visit her website at www.jodeeblanco.com.

17

Rose Carmen Goldberg

Rose Carmen Goldberg is a public interest lawyer and policy advocate. She is a nationally-recognized leader in veterans' rights with a focus on advancing justice for underserved veterans, including veterans with mental health conditions, veteran sexual assault survivors, Native American veterans, and immigrant veterans. Rose's decade-plus of public interest work spans academia, state service, legal aid, and all branches of the federal government. Currently, she is Associate Director of Policy and Programs at Stanford Law School's Deborah L. Rhode Center, managing programs and conducting original research to make the legal system more accessible and equitable, with a special interest in veterans' access to justice. She also teaches the next generation of veterans law attorneys as Director of the Veterans Law Practicum at UC Berkeley School of Law. Previously, she led high-impact litigation and policy advocacy affecting millions of people at the California Attorney General's Office. Her work focused primarily on gun violence prevention and veterans' rights. She is a graduate of Yale Law School.

Why did I want to interview Rose Carmen Goldberg?

As a lawyer fighting to institute significant social change, I knew Rose would have an interesting story to share about what it is like to be a lawyer and navigate the legal system despite the many challenges and risks lawyers face. Understanding that our justice system isn't always equitable and fair, I felt Rose could provide some insight into how she works to combat the faults in our justice system. Connecting with clients and being their voice makes lawyers strong, confident figures with a lot of pressure and courage to combat a system that won't always work in a client's favor. I wanted to recognize the extremity of the sometimes unfair nature of the justice system through the lens of a lawyer.

Ashley: What is a challenging experience you have faced, and how did overcoming it make you stronger?

Rose: Growing up, not in my wildest imagination would I ever have thought I'd become a lawyer. But I am one now.

Not only are there no lawyers in my family, since before I was born, and continuing today, my family has been represented by pro bono attorneys. I viewed lawyers as lofty creatures who spoke a powerful language my family and I didn't understand. I viewed my family as vulnerable, at the mercy of the whims of this power.

Based on this experience, I came to see a false dichotomy. On one side, there were lawyers living at a personal remove from the law but with the power to help those ensnared by it in ways that could change their lives. On the other, there were people for whom the law was not an abstract exercise and whose wellbeing depends on it. They, so I thought, didn't have the knowledge or authority to achieve justice on their own. I saw myself in this second camp.

Over time, my mind started to open to the power of lived experience in the law. Being personally impacted by the legal system grew into a fire to fight for other people's dignity. At first, I channeled this into non-legal work, still feeling that the legal profession was not a place for people like me. I started a GED program in a penitentiary, did HIV/AIDS work in Uganda and Russia, and worked for the U.S. federal government to improve end-of-life care for those with six months or less left to live, among other things.

In doing this work, I kept running into the law. For instance, statutes and regulations are what ultimately control access to health-care in the U.S., including at the end of life. And I felt a growing urge to engage in advocacy, going straight to the legal heart of the social problems I was trying to tackle. Underlying this, I also wanted to use my voice in a different, more personal way. After many conversations with friends who had gone to law school, I finally realized that I belonged, too. They helped me recognize that my insider's view of the law was a strength, not a weakness.

Law school was still an adjustment. Unlike some who go to law school because they "like to argue," I was drawn in by a personal commitment to fairness. At first, there were parts of law school that I found alienating, such as subjects that used the "us/them" power dichotomy I'd only recently overcome myself. In addition, learning about how inhumane the legal system can be could be was disheartening. But before long, I found my home in law school. The turning point was when I started working in my law school's veterans' legal services clinic. I was drawn to the clinic because of its focus on disability and women's rights and the opportunity to help those who would otherwise go without needed legal assistance. When I heard about the clinic's work advocating on behalf of military sexual assault survivors, for instance, I felt that fire inside me, burning since childhood, ignite. But I still thought it might be a one semester experiment. Representing clients—literally sitting on the other side of the table—just seemed too close to home.

But after just a few meetings with my first client, I was hooked. I'd seen my own family nervously carry worn printouts of laws in their pockets. I'd heard their voices shake and seen their sleep disrupted while waiting for decisions. My understanding better equipped me to help my client. And doing so was so rewarding. Plus, I simply enjoyed spending time with my client. I knew that whatever followed in my legal career, this experience would somehow be foundational. It was.

After law school, I followed my dream to turn my veterans clinic experience into a full-time job. Thanks to a generous fellowship, I built a new program for veterans where I grew up, in the California Bay Area, integrating legal and mental health services. My veteran clients had been kicked out of the military due to racism, mental health discrimination, or after experiencing sexual assault. Because of their discharges, they were cut off from critical healthcare and disability benefits. In the ensuing years of representing veterans, my clients shared intimate aspects of their lives with me. Sometimes including traumas they'd experienced in the military they'd never told another living soul. To me, the relationships I built with my clients were sacred.

I understood the depth of trust required for them to share their stories and the risk of pain that came with the possibility of losing their case. To be able to come full circle and give the kind of pro bono legal assistance my family received—what greater gift is there than that?

I hope that other women lawyers recognize what took me years to see: that strengths in the practice of law come in different shapes and sizes. And that power can grow from personal challenges.

What I learned from interviewing Rose Carmen Goldberg

After our interview, and knowing Rose and her family had been at the mercy of the legal system, I felt a deep connection to her story. It was inspiring to hear how her upbringing, which involved being at the mercy of the justice system, shifted her mentality as a lawyer and gave her a better understanding of her clients' positions. Sometimes challenging moments in our lives inadvertently help us later on, giving us a more profound perspective on the struggles faced by others. Struggles can help us better understand our own personal growth and career, as was the case with Rose.

Final Thoughts

Upon finishing *The Challenges We Faced, The Women We Became*, I feel both the pain and resilience that shine through the stories that these women shared and a deep sense of hope for the challenges that they were able to overcome. Hope that these experiences did not define their lives and that they have managed to persevere and live meaningful, impactful lives despite immense challenges. Hope that by sharing these stories, we can create a world where diverse thoughts are encouraged and better understood. Hope that the next generation, including my generation, will continue to break barriers and redefine possibilities. And lastly, hope that we will use these lessons to better ourselves and understand the impact that our individual actions can have on others, thereby fostering inclusivity and equity.

While conducting these interviews, I grew as a young woman looking to navigate the challenges I may face in my career and personal life, and I better learned how to lead a life that is truly impactful. I now understand that acceptance and moving forward minimizes the control our challenges have over us and that stories give the inspiration needed to help others achieve this. Sharing stories also acts as a marker of where we are in the world. What were the kinds of challenges women faced during this time period? How can we improve in the future? Documenting womens' stories in society today only leaves us with more room for improvement and change moving forward. Once we process what happens around us and the injustices that need societal change, our personal identity can be stronger than ever. As I look back on each interview, I find myself tearing up with the realization of how deeply these interviews helped me feel more ready than ever to approach the world and understand the power of individual stories. Each woman I interviewed serves as a role model for society. My hope is for this book to be your guide to the diverse challenges you may face, empowering you to take action in your own life, whether through your own personal growth or for society as a whole.

As a young journalist looking to make a meaningful contribution to improving the lives of others and to bring about change to societal injustices, I've noticed more than ever that diverse perspectives are constantly needed. If we do not understand issues from a global standpoint, it makes it harder to see the whole picture and understand the mark of history. We are not learning from the past and growing as a world if we are not constantly looking to create peace and make compromises. Peaceful discourse and having a profound and broad understanding of societal issues throughout the world will help contribute towards decision-making and policies that promote empathy and justice.

Towards the end of this journey of interviewing women from diverse backgrounds, the main takeaway I had was how each woman bounced back from their challenge and was able to heal from it. When we come to terms with what has happened to us and reverse our obstacles into something to uplift others, we are no longer running from what we have faced. Instead, we're using it to influence our role in society. Confident and educated, these women have taught me—and now hopefully you—that the cycle of reform is continuous, and the first step in improving this cycle is connecting with others and understanding the perspectives they hold.

These conversations do not end here—the lessons learned and commonality of the themes can hopefully serve as a reminder throughout daily life that through collective effort to survive the obstacles we face, we also learn valuable lessons that can have a lasting impact on ourselves and others.

These interviews covered a broad array of injustices and responses by strong women who did not let injustices define them. Now, it is our turn to act. The fire has been ignited within us to further the work that remains; this can be through supporting policies that promote gender equality, mentoring the next generation of leaders, or simply listening and learning from one another. We all have a role to play.

Here are the biggest lessons I've learned from this process: Constantly question the world around you—look for underlying injustice and speak up. Learn from others' perspectives, and let your thoughts continue to grow and even be challenged by the stories you hear. And most importantly: Recognize that everyone has a significant story to share.

Photo by Natalie Cartz

Ashley Barcroft is a young writer and journalist from New York. She was a student at the School of the New York Times in the Investigative Journalism program and has served as co-president of Amnesty International at her school. Ashley is passionate about social justice and sharing diverse stories to initiate change. When she's not writing and investigating, Ashley enjoys skiing, sculpting, teaching art, and hiking.

www.ingramcontent.com/pod-product-compliance
Lightning Source LLC
Chambersburg PA
CBHW031420120626
46545CB00006B/2203